FISH COOKBOOK

SMOKING FISH AND SEAFOOD

ROGER MURPHY

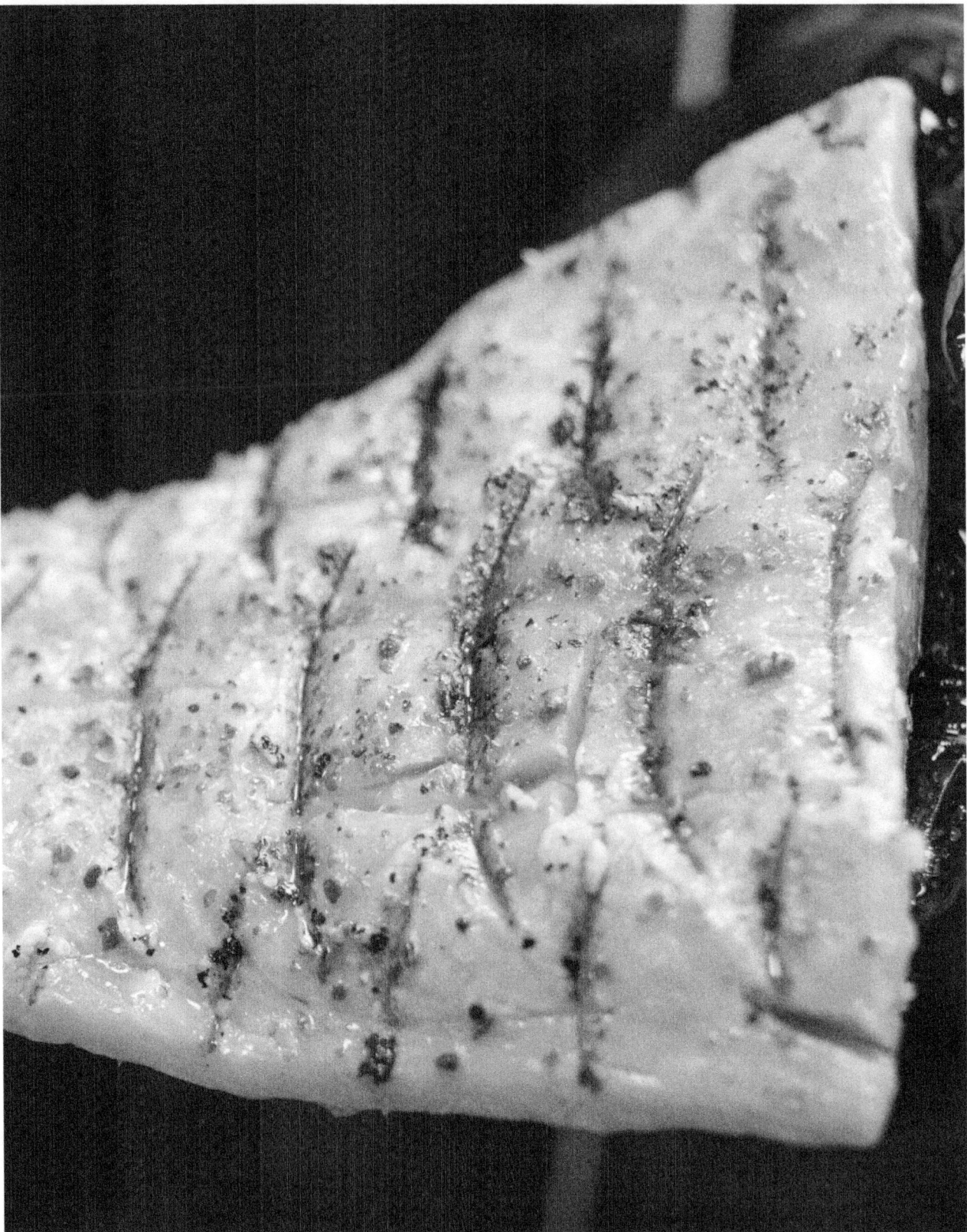

CONTENTS

CHAPTER 1: SALMON 10
CHAPTER 2: TROUT 21
CHAPTER 3: TUNA 34
CHAPTER 4: SEAFOOD 46
CHAPTER 5: MORE FISH.................60
CHAPTER 6: SAUCES 76
CHAPTER 7: SMOKING MEAT 88
CHAPTER 8: FOOD SAFETY 102
RECIPES INDEX.................109

GRAB YOUR SMOKING GEAR, AND GET READY FOR SOME DELICIOUS MEALS IN THE OUTDOORS.

INTRODUCTION

With clear and concise instructions, this book shows you how to get the most out of your smoker. This book provides detailed instructions on how to smoke salmon, trout, tuna, seafood, and more, as well as tips on selecting the best cuts of fish and choosing the correct wood chips for flavor. Although the cookbook contains irresistible recipes guaranteed to please, including classic favorites alder smoked salmon, and spicy tuna, you'll also find exciting dishes like smoked lobster tails, catfish fillets, and even smoked king crab legs. Are you looking to perfect your smoked fish game? With clear instructions and easy-to-follow steps, this book will help you take your smoking to the next level. Look no further than this fantastic smoking fish cookbook with everything you need to know about smoking, including how to choose the right smoker, what cuts of fish work best, and how to create flavorful recipes that impress you, your friends, and your family. Whether you're a beginner or a seasoned pro, this cookbook is a must-have for any smoker's library!

SMOKING

Smoking is generally used as one of the cooking methods nowadays. With modern cooking techniques, food enriched in protein, such as meat, would spoil if cooked for extended periods. Whereas, Smoking is a low & slow process of cooking meat. Where there is smoke, there is a flavor. With white smoke, you can boost the taste of your food. In addition to this statement, you can also preserve the nutrition in the food. Smoking is flexible & one of the oldest techniques of making food. You must brush the marinade over your food while you cook and let the miracle happen. The only thing you need to do is to add a handful of fresh wood chips when required. Just taste your regular grilled and smoked meat, and you will find the difference. Remember one thing, i.e., "Smoking is an art." With a bit of time & practice, even you can become an expert. Once you become an expert in smoking techniques, you will never look for other cooking techniques. To find which smoking technique works for you, you must experiment with different woods & cooking methods. Just cook the meat over an indirect heat source & cook it for hours. When smoking your meats, you must let the smoke escape & move around.

ALDER SMOKED APPLE CIDER SALMON

CHAPTER 1

SALMON

- **ALDER SMOKED APPLE CIDER SALMON** 12
- **APRICOT SMOKED SALMON** 13
- **ASIAN COHO SMOKED SALMON** 15
- **PESTO TOPPED SALMON** 16
- **SMOKED SALMON NUGGETS** 17
- **BROWN SUGAR SMOKED SALMON** 19
- **MAPLE AND ORANGE SMOKED SALMON** 20

ALDER SMOKED APPLE CIDER SALMON
(TOTAL COOK TIME 4 HOURS 5 MINUTES)

INGREDIENTS FOR 4-6 SERVINGS

THE FISH

- 1 wild salmon fillet, center cut, skin-on, boned (1½ -lb, 0.7-kgs)
- Coarsely ground black pepper – 1 teaspoon

THE MARINADE

- Apple cider – 1½ cups
- Gin – 2 tablespoons
- 1 piece star anise, broken
- 1 bay leaf, roughly crumbled

THE CURE

- Kosher salt – ½ cup
- Dark brown sugar – ¼ cup
- Barbecue rub, of choice – 2 teaspoons

THE SMOKE

- When you are ready to cook, with the lid open, set the grill to smoke for 4-5 minutes, until the fire is well established
- Preheat with the lid closed for 10-15 minutes, to 200°F (95°C)

METHOD

1. First, gently rinse the salmon under cold running water and using kitchen paper, pat dry.
2. In a Ziplock bag, combine the apple cider with the gin, star anise, and bay leaf.
3. Add the salmon to the bag and transfer to the fridge, overnight.
4. Take the salmon out of the bag and discard the marinade.
5. Using kitchen paper towel, dry the salmon.
6. Next, prepare the cure. In a bowl, combine the salt with the dark brown sugar and barbecue rub.
7. Pour half of the cure into a shallow dish.
8. Lay the salmon, skin side facing downwards on top of the cure.
9. Scatter the other half of the cure over the top and cover with kitchen wrap. Transfer to the fridge for no more than 60-90 minutes.

CONTINUED

10. Remove the fish from the mixture and using kitchen paper towel, pat dry.
11. Season with black pepper.
12. Arrange the salmon, skin side facing downwards on the grill grate and cook for 60 minutes until it reaches an internal temperature of 150°F (65°C) and flakes easily when using a fork. Set to one side to cool.
13. When cool, flip the fillet over and carefully remove its skin.
14. Serve and enjoy.

APRICOT SMOKED SALMON
(TOTAL COOK TIME 12 HOURS)

INGREDIENTS FOR 4-6 SERVINGS

THE FISH

- 1 wild salmon fillet, center cut, skin-on, boned (1½ -lb, 0.7-kgs)
- Non-iodized rock salt
- Apricot syrup, to baste

THE SMOKE

- Alder wood chips work well this recipe.
- When you are ready to cook, with the lid open, set the grill to smoke for 4-5 minutes, or until the fire is well established.
- Preheat, with the lid closed for 10-15 minutes, to 120°F (50°C).

METHOD

1. Liberally season the fleshy part of the salmon with rock salt and set aside to stand, overnight.
2. Rinse the fish under cold running water, pat dry using kitchen paper towel and allow to air dry for 60 minutes.
3. Lay the fish on racks and baste with apricot syrup. Place on the smoker.
4. Baste 4-5 times with apricot syrup during the smoking process, smoking until the fish in its thickest part reaches an internal temperature of 150°F (65°C). This should take between 3-5 hours.

ASIAN COHO SMOKED SALMON

ASIAN COHO SMOKED SALMON
(TOTAL COOK TIME 8 HOURS 55 MINUTES)

INGREDIENTS FOR 4 SERVINGS

THE FISH

- Wild coho salmon (1-lb, 0.5-kgs)

THE MARINADE

- Boiling water – 1 cup
- Diamond crystal kosher salt – 1½ teaspoons
- Coconut aminos – 1 cup
- 1 garlic clove, peeled and grated
- Dijon mustard – 1 tablespoon
- Chili flakes – 1 teaspoon

THE SMOKE

- Set your grill to smoke. You are ready to cook as soon as white smoke appears

METHOD

1. In a bowl, combine the water along with the salt, stirring to dissolve the salt. Set aside to stand at room temperature, to cool.
2. Add ¼ cup of the coconut aminos, along with the garlic, Dijon mustard and chili flakes, stirring well to combine.
3. Rinse the salmon under cold running water and pat dry with kitchen paper towel.
4. Transfer the salmon to a Ziploc bag and add the marinade. Squeeze out as much excess air from the bag as is possible, zip the bag tightly closed and transfer to the fridge for between 3-4 hours.
5. Take the salmon out of the bag, and pat dry with kitchen towel. Lay the salmon on a baking sheet lined with parchment paper. Discard the marinade. Transfer to the fridge uncovered for 2-3 hours until a pellicle* forms.
6. Transfer the baking sheet and salmon to the grill and with the lid closed, smoke for 45 minutes. Do not disturb the salmon at any time during the smoking process.

CONTINUED

7. In the meantime, in a small pan, heat the remaining coconut aminos over moderate to low heat. Reduce the aminos to half of their original volume and put to one side.
8. Using kitchen paper, wipe off any albumin and baste the salmon with the reduced aminos. Turn the heat up to 225°F (110°C) and smoke for an additional 40-45 minutes, or until it reaches an internal temperature of 145°F (65°C). Baste the salmon with the reduced aminos every 15-20 minutes, and just before serving.
9. Serve and enjoy.

*A pellicle is a coating or skin of protein which naturally forms on the surface of fish/meat/poultry. It allows smoke to adhere to the surface of the fish better during the smoking process for a more intense and full-bodied flavor.

PESTO TOPPED SALMON
(TOTAL COOK TIME 1 HOUR 5 MINUTES)

INGREDIENTS FOR 4 SERVINGS

THE FISH
- 1 large salmon fillet

THE INGREDIENTS
- Olive oil – 1 tablespoon
- Salt and black pepper, as needed, to season
- Basil pesto, store-bought, any brand – 1 cup

THE SMOKE
- Set the smoker to 250°F (120°C)

METHOD
1. Place the salmon fillet on a sheet pan and drizzle with olive oil. Season the fish with salt and black pepper.
2. Spoon the basil pesto over the salmon.
3. Smoke the fish for 60 minutes until it registers an internal temperature of 145°F (65°C).
4. Remove from the smoker and serve.

SMOKED SALMON NUGGETS

(TOTAL COOK TIME 4 HOURS 20 MINUTES)

INGREDIENTS FOR 4 SERVINGS

THE FISH

- Whole fresh salmon fillets, skinned, rinsed, patted dry, and cut into 1-in (2.5-cm) cubes. Total weight (4-lb, 1.4-kg)

THE BRINE

- Brown sugar – 6 cups
- Coarse sea salt – 2 cups
- Ground garlic powder – 2 tablespoons
- Ground onion powder – 2 tablespoons
- Freshly ground black pepper - 1 tablespoon
- Ground cayenne – 1 teaspoon

THE SMOKE

- Preheat your smoker to 120°F (50°C) increasing to 180°F (85°C) during the cooking process. See instructions Step 4
- Alder wood chips are a good choice for this recipe

METHOD

1. In a bowl, combine the brine ingredients (brown sugar, salt, garlic powder, onion powder, black pepper, and cayenne). Toss the cubes of salmon in the brines, making sure it is well and evenly coated. Transfer to the fridge for 6-8 hours.
2. Take the salmon out of the fridge, and with cold water, wash thoroughly.
3. Place the salmon cubes on a smoker rack, making sure they are not touching, and allow to air dry until a pellicle forms on the fish. You can also use a fan to help with air circulation.
4. Place the smoker rack in the smoker and cook for 4 hours. You will need to incase the temperature by 20°F (5°C) every 60 minutes.
5. Remove the fish from the smoker and serve.

BROWN SUGAR SMOKED SALMON

(TOTAL COOK TIME 2 HOURS 5 MINUTES)

INGREDIENTS FOR 4-6 SERVINGS

THE FISH

- Fresh salmon (2-lb, 0.9-kgs)

THE RUB

- Kosher salt – 1 teaspoon
- Black pepper – 1 teaspoon
- Dill – 1 teaspoon
- Brown sugar – 2 tablespoons

THE SMOKE

- Preheat the smoker to between 250°F-275°F (120°C-135°C)
- Choose either oak, cherry wood or pecan wood chips

METHOD

1. In a bowl, combine the salt with the black pepper followed by the dill and sugar.
2. Gently pat the mixture all over the top of the salmon and transfer to the fridge for 60 minutes.
3. Smoke the salmon for 60 minutes, until it reaches an internal temperature of 145°F (65°C).
4. Enjoy.

MAPLE AND ORANGE SMOKED SALMON
(TOTAL COOK TIME 20 HOURS 10 MINUTES)

INGREDIENTS FOR 8 SERVINGS

THE FISH

- 8 salmon fillets (6-oz, 160-gms each)

THE MARINADE

- Cool water – 4 cups
- Maple syrup – 1 cup
- Brown sugar – ½ cup
- Kosher salt – ⅓ cup
- Zest of 1 medium orange

THE GLAZE

- Maple syrup – ½ cup
- Freshly squeezed orange juice – ¼ cup

THE SMOKE

- Preheat the smoker to 170°F (75°C)

METHOD

1. In a glass casserole dish, combine the water with the syrup, brown sugar, salt, and orange zest, and stir until the salt is entirely dissolved.
2. Submerge the portions of salmon in the mixture, cover with a lid and transfer to the fridge, overnight.
3. Remove the fish from the mixture and place on a rack set over a baking sheet.
4. Return the fish, overnight to the fridge in order to form a pellicle*.
5. In a bowl, combine the maple syrup with the fresh orange juice and put to one side.
6. Lay the salmon the grill grates, skin side facing downwards and smoke for between 3-4 hours until the internal temperature of the fish registers 145°F (65°C). Remember to liberally brush the fish with the glaze every 60 minutes or so, while it smokes.
7. Flake the salmon and enjoy either warm or cold.

*A pellicle is a coating or skin of protein which naturally forms on the surface of fish/meat/poultry. It allows smoke to adhere to the surface of the fish better during the smoking process for a more intense and full-bodied flavor.

CITRUS STUFFED RAINBOW TROUT WITH BROWN BUTTER

CHAPTER 2

TROUT

CITRUS STUFFED RAINBOW TROUT WITH BROWN BUTTER 23
SMOKED RAINBOW TROUT WITH BROWN SUGAR ...24
SMOKED TROUT WITH BEET AND POTATO HASH 26
FRESH TROUT, CREAM CHEESE, AND RED ONION BAGUETTE...28
SMOKED TROUT WITH GARLIC, LEMON, AND BASIL 30
SMOKED TROUT WITH GREEK FETA SALAD 31
SMOKED RAINBOW TROUT WITH LEMON DILL SAUCE 33

CITRUS STUFFED RAINBOW TROUT WITH BROWN BUTTER
(TOTAL COOK TIME 35 MINUTES)

INGREDIENTS FOR 2-4 SERVINGS

THE FISH
- 1 whole rainbow trout, cleaned

THE DIP
- Butter – 4 tablespoons
- Squeeze of lemon juice
- Salt – 1 tablespoon
- Chipotle pepper powder – 1 teaspoon
- 2 lemon slices
- 2 orange slices
- 3 bay leaves
- 4 sprigs thyme
- 1 garlic bulb, cut into quarters

THE SMOKE
- Set the grill to smoke with the lid open; establish the fire for 4-5 minutes.
- Set the temperature to 400°F (210°C) and with the lid closed preheat for 10-15 minutes.

METHOD
1. Over moderate heat, add the butter to a small pan and heat until it begins to foam and brown.
2. When the foam subsides, and the butter is golden, remove from the heat.
3. Squeeze in a drop of lemon juice, to prevent browning and set to one side.
4. Arrange a sheet of foil, which is 3-ins, 7.60-cms longer on each end than the fish.
5. Drizzle the surface and cavity of the fish with the browned butter and season with salt and chipotle pepper powder.
6. Stuff the cavity with the remaining ingredients (lemon slices, orange slices, bay leaves, thyme sprigs, and garlic) and fold the foil to form a packet.
7. Lay the packet on the grill grate and cook for 15 minutes, until the internal temperature in the thickest part of the fish registers 145°F (65°C).

SMOKED RAINBOW TROUT WITH BROWN SUGAR
(TOTAL COOK TIME 3 HOURS 15 MINUTES)

INGREDIENTS FOR 4-6 SERVINGS

THE FISH

- 2 rainbow trout fillets, boned

THE RUB

- Brown sugar – ⅓ cup
- Salt – 1 teaspoon
- Garlic powder – 1 teaspoon
- Onion powder – 1 teaspoon
- Ground black pepper – ½ teaspoon
- Ground cayenne pepper – ½ teaspoon

THE SMOKE

- Start the smoker and using alder wood chips, bring the smoker to 250°F (120°C)

METHOD

1. Lay the trout fillets side by side on the smoker rack ensuring they do not touch one another.
2. In a bowl, combine the brown sugar with the salt, garlic powder, onion powder, black pepper, and cayenne pepper. Rub the mixture on both sides of each trout fillet.
3. Place the fish in the smoker and cook for between 2-3 hours, until the fish registers an internal temperature of 140°F (60°C).
4. Serve straight away

FRESH TROUT, CREAM CHEESE, AND RED ONION BAGUETTE

SMOKED TROUT WITH BEET AND POTATO HASH

(TOTAL COOK TIME 4 HOURS 30 MINUTES)

INGREDIENTS FOR 4-6 SERVINGS

THE FISH

- Whole trout (2-lb, 0.9-kgs)

THE BRINE

- Water – 4 cups
- Sea salt – 1 cup
- Brown sugar – ½ cup
- Zest of 1 medium lemon
- 4 bay leaves
- Black peppercorns – 1 tablespoon
- Ice water – 4 cups

THE HASH

- Olive oil – 1 tablespoon
- Beets, peeled, diced – ½ cup
- New potatoes, halved – ½ cup
- 2 green onions, thinly sliced
- 4 medium eggs

THE SMOKE

- When you are ready to cook, with the lid open, start the grill on smoke to establish the fire, for between 4-6 minutes.
- With the temperature set on smoke, preheat for 12-15 minutes.

METHOD

1. First, prepare the brine. In a pan, combine the water with the salt, brown sugar, lemon zest, bay leaves, and peppercorns. Place the pan over moderate to high heat and cook until the salt and sugar entirely dissolve.
2. Remove the pan from the heat and allow to steep for 15 minutes at room temperature.
3. Pour the mixture over the iced water, and allow to cool completely

CONTINUED

4. Once sufficiently cooked, pour over the fish, cover and transfer to the fridge for a couple of hours.
5. Take the fish out of the brine and discard the brine.
6. Under cold running water, rinse the fish and pat dry with kitchen paper towel.
7. Lay the fish on a cool rack and place in the fridge overnight, to a form a pellicle*.
8. When you are ready to smoke, lay the fish directly on the grilling grate and smoke for 60-90 minutes, until the fish flakes.
9. Turn the temperature up to 375°F(190°C), and with the lid closed, continue cooking for 10-15 minutes.
10. Over moderate to high heat, in a skillet heat the oil.
11. Add the beets to the hot oil and cook until almost fork-tender, 8-10 minutes.
12. Add the potatoes to the skillet and cook until fork tender, approximately 10 minutes.
13. Add the flaked trout followed by the green onions and cook until the fish is warmed through, for 4-5 minutes.
14. Form 4 wells in the potato hash.
15. Crack an egg into each of the wells and transfer the skillet to the grill, cooking until the whites are entirely set but the yolks runny, 4-6 minutes.
16. Serve.

*A pellicle is a coating or skin of protein which naturally forms on the surface of fish/meat/poultry. It allows smoke to adhere to the surface of the fish better during the smoking process for a more intense and full-bodied flavor.

FRESH TROUT, CREAM CHEESE, AND RED ONION BAGUETTE

(TOTAL COOK TIME 2 HOURS)

INGREDIENTS FOR 6 SERVINGS

THE FISH

- 6 rainbow trout fillets
- French baguette, split, as needed, to serve
- Cream cheese, as needed, to serve
- Red onion slices, as needed, to serve, optional

THE BRINE

- Water, cooled – 4 cups
- Brown sugar – 2 tablespoons
- Kosher salt – 2 tablespoons

THE SMOKE

- Preheat your smoker to 180°F (85°C)
- Choose your favorite wood chips for this recipe

METHOD

1. In a bowl, combine the water with brown sugar and salt. Stir well to dissolve the sugar and salt.
2. Place the fish skin side facing up in the brine and set aside for 15 minutes.
3. Remove the fish from the brine and lay the fish directly on the smoker grates.
4. Close the smoker's lid and smoke for 1½ -2 hours until the fish registers an internal temperature of 145°F (65°C) and until the trout flakes easily when using a fork.
5. Remove the trout from the heat and chop into pieces.
6. Spread the cut side of the baguette(s) with cream cheese, top with trout and red onion slices, and enjoy.

SMOKED TROUT WITH GREEK FETA SALAD

SMOKED TROUT WITH GARLIC, LEMON, AND BASIL
(TOTAL COOK TIME 50 MINUTES)

INGREDIENTS FOR 6 SERVINGS

THE FISH
- 6 whole trout

THE SEASONING
- Garlic rub, of choice – 2 teaspoons
- 12 sprigs of fresh basil
- 3 medium lemons, halved, seeded
- Virgin olive oil

THE SMOKE
- When you are ready to begin cooking, with the lid open, set the grill to smoke and establish the fire, this will take between 4-5 minutes.
- Set the temperature to 450°F (235°C) and with the lid closed preheat for between 10-15 minutes

METHOD

1. Season the middle cavity of each trout with the garlic rub.
2. Add 2 basil sprigs to each cavity along with the lemon halves.
3. Using kitchen twine, tie the trout closed.
4. Rub the trout with olive oil and cook for 15 minutes each side.
5. Serve straight away.

SMOKED TROUT WITH GREEK FETA SALAD

(TOTAL COOK TIME 14 HOURS 10 MINUTES)

INGREDIENTS FOR 4 SERVINGS

THE FISH

- 1 large trout, cleaned, pin boned, filleted, cut into 4 fillets

THE CURE

- Caster sugar – ½ cup
- Sea salt – 1 cup

THE SALAD

- Feta 7 oz (200g), roughly chopped
- White balsamic vinegar – 1 tablespoon
- Extra virgin olive oil – 3 tablespoons
- 2 shallots, peeled, sliced into rings
- Cooked beetroot, coarsely chopped – 1 cup
- Handful of watercress
- Sea salt and black pepper

THE SMOKE

- Use oak wood chips for smoking.
- When you are ready to cook, add the chips to your smoker. Light the chips, with the lid down preheat for 10-15 minutes. Set the temperature to 225°F (110°C)

METHOD

1. First, prepare the cure. In a bowl, combine the sugar with the salt and divide into 4 equally-sized portions.
2. Lay a sheet of kitchen wrap on a clean worktop. Arrange another sheet on top.
3. Scatter 1 portion of the salt-sugar mixture in a line across the middle of the wrap.
4. Lay 1 trout fillet, skin side facing downwards on the line of sugar-salt.
5. Scatter another single portion of salt-sugar over the fish fillet before wrapping in kitchen wrap.
6. Repeat the process with the remaining trout and chill in the fridge for between 12-14 hours.

CONTINUED

7. Once the trout is cured, remove the kitchen wrap and lightly brush with the salt-sugar.
8. Under cold running water, rinse the fish before patting dry with kitchen paper.
9. Lay the trout, skin side facing downwards in the middle of the grill grate. Cover with the lid and smoke for between 60-90 minutes. You will need to regularly check that the chips are not burning.
10. When the trout is cooked through, take it out of the smoker and set it to one side.
11. In the meantime, prepare the salad. In a bowl, whisk the vinegar with the oil.
12. Season with salt and pepper, to taste.
13. Arrange the rings of shallot, chopped beetroot and crumbled feta on a serving plate.
14. Flake the cooked trout over the top, garnish with cress and drizzle with dressing.

SMOKED RAINBOW TROUT WITH LEMON DILL SAUCE
(TOTAL COOK TIME 1 HOUR)

INGREDIENTS FOR 4-6 SERVINGS

THE FISH
- 2 boneless rainbow trout fillets, scaled

THE MARINADE
- Fresh ginger, grated – 2 teaspoons
- Maple syrup – ½ cup
- Zest and juice of 1 lemon
- Rice wine vinegar – 2 teaspoons
- Fresh cracked black pepper

THE SAUCE
- Mayonnaise – 1 cup
- Juice and zest of 1 lemon
- Fresh dill, chopped – 1 tablespoon
- Wholegrain mustard – 2 teaspoons
- Black pepper, to taste

THE SMOKE
- After marinating, when ready to cook, preheat your smoker to 220°F (105°C).
- We recommend hickory wood for this recipe

METHOD
1. First, prepare the marinade. Combine all the ingredients (ginger, maple syrup, lemon zest, juice, rice wine vinegar, and black pepper) in a bowl.
2. Add the fish fillets to a large ziplock bag and pour in the marinade. Seal the bag and chill for half an hour.
3. In the meantime, prepare the sauce. Add the mayonnaise, lemon juice, zest, dill, mustard, and black pepper to a bowl and stir to combine. Cover and chill until ready to serve.
4. Take the trout out of the marinade and place it in the smoker. Cook for 20-30 minutes
5. Take the fish out of the smoker and serve with the prepared sauce.

CHAPTER 3

TUNA

ASIAN ORANGE AND TUNA SALAD 36
HOT AND SPICY TUNA 37
LEMON-PEPPER AHI TUNA STEAKS 39
MAPLE-SMOKED TUNA 40
THAI TUNA FISHCAKES 42
SMOKEY TUNA TACOS 43
TUNA STEAKS 45

ASIAN ORANGE AND TUNA SALAD

(TOTAL COOK TIME 1 HOUR 45 MINUTES)

INGREDIENTS FOR 4-6 SERVINGS

THE FISH

- Albacore tuna loin (1-lb, 0.5-kgs)

THE MARINADE

- Kosher salt – 2 tablespoons
- Brown sugar – ¼ cup
- Water – 2 cups
- Soy sauce – 2 tablespoons

THE SALAD

- 1 orange bell pepper, seeded and chopped
- 3 scallions, chopped
- 1 large orange, peeled and segmented
- Mayonnaise – 3 tablespoons
- Sriracha sauce – 2 teaspoons
- Soy sauce – 1 tablespoon
- Zest and juice of 1 lime
- Sesame oil – 1 teaspoon
- Powdered ginger – 1 teaspoon

THE SMOKE

- Load smoker with alder briquettes and preheat to 140°F (60°C).

METHOD

1. First, prepare the marinade. Combine all of the marinade ingredients (salt, sugar, water, soy sauce) in a bowl.
2. Slice the tuna into 3-ins (7.5-cm) pieces and add to the marinade. Gently press the filets down into the liquid to aid absorption. Chill for half an hour.
3. Place the marinated fish in the smoker and smoke for approximately an hour.

CONTINUED

4. Take the fish out of the smoker and flake into large pieces using a fork.
5. Add the flaked tuna to a serving bowl along with the bell pepper, scallions, and orange. Gently toss to combine.
6. In a small bowl, whisk together the mayonnaise, sriracha, soy sauce, zest and lime juice, sesame oil, and ginger until combined. Drizzle the mixture over the tuna/orange salad and toss again gently to coat.
7. Keep chilled until ready to serve.

HOT AND SPICY TUNA
(TOTAL COOK TIME 1 HOUR 10 MINUTES)

INGREDIENTS FOR 4-6 SERVINGS

THE FISH
- Albacore tuna loin (1-lb, 0.5-kgs)

THE MARINADE
- Chili flakes, crushed – 1 tablespoon
- Brown sugar – ¼ cup
- Zest and juice of 1 lime
- Kosher salt – 2 tablespoons
- Soy sauce – 1 tablespoon
- Sriracha sauce – 2 tablespoon
- Water – 2 cups

THE SMOKE
- Preheat smoker to 140°F (60°C).

METHOD
1. First, prepare the marinade. Combine all of the marinade ingredients (chili flakes, brown sugar, zest and lime juice, kosher salt, soy sauce, sriracha sauce, and water) in a large bowl.
2. Slice the loin into pieces and add to the marinade. Gently press the fish down into the liquid to aid absorption. Cover and chill for half an hour.
3. Take the tuna out of the marinade, pat dry using kitchen paper towel and transfer to aluminum cooking trays.
4. Place the trays in the smoker and smoke for just over half an hour.
5. Serve straight away.

MAPLE-SMOKED TUNA

LEMON-PEPPER AHI TUNA STEAKS

(TOTAL COOK TIME 10 HOURS 10 MINUTES)

INGREDIENTS FOR 2 SERVINGS

THE FISH

- 2 ahi tuna steaks

THE RUB

- Brown sugar – 1 tablespoon
- Kosher salt – 1 tablespoon
- Olive oil – 4 tablespoons
- Lemon pepper seasoning – to taste
- Juice of ½ a lemon
- Fresh parsley, chopped – 1 tablespoon

THE SMOKE

- After overnight marinating, the following day, load smoker with cherry/peach wood and preheat to 190°F (90°C).

METHOD

1. First, prepare the rub. Combine the sugar and salt in a small bowl. Rub the mixture over both sides of each tuna steak and chill overnight.
2. The following day, brush the excess sugar and salt of the steaks and drizzle each with a little olive oil. Next, sprinkle with lemon pepper seasoning and finish by squeezing over a little lemon juice.
3. Put the fish in the smoker for just over 90-105 minutes.
4. Sprinkle the steaks with fresh parsley and serve straight away.

MAPLE-SMOKED TUNA

(TOTAL COOK TIME 9 HOURS 45 MINUTES)

INGREDIENTS FOR 6-8 SERVINGS

THE FISH

- 4 tuna fillets (1-lb, 0.5-kgs each)

THE MARINADE

- Mustard seed – 1 tablespoon
- Dried dill – 1 tablespoon
- Black pepper – 1 teaspoon
- Salt – 3 tablespoon
- 2 bay leaves
- Brown sugar – ½ cup
- Water – 4 cups

THE SMOKE

- After overnight marinating, the following day, load smoker with maple briquettes and preheat to 220°F (110°C). Ensure the grill racks are well oiled.

METHOD

1. First, make the marinade. Combine all of the marinade ingredients (mustard seed, dill, black pepper, salt, bay leaves, brown sugar, and water) in a bowl. Stir well until the sugar and salt dissolve completely.
2. Add the tuna to the marinade, cover tightly with plastic wrap and chill overnight.
3. The following day, take the fish out of the marinade and pat dry using kitchen paper towel.
4. Place the tuna in the smoker on oiled racks and smoke for just over 90 minutes.
5. Serve straight away.

THAI TUNA FISHCAKES

THAI TUNA FISHCAKES

(TOTAL COOK TIME 2 HOURS 10 MINUTES)

INGREDIENTS FOR 4-6 SERVINGS

THE FISH

- Albacore tuna loin (1-lb, 0.5-kgs)

THE MARINADE

- Kosher salt – 1 tablespoon
- Brown sugar – 3 tablespoons
- Water – 1 cup
- Soy sauce – 1 tablespoon

THE FISH CAKES

- 2 stick celery, finely chopped
- Breadcrumbs – 1 cup
- 1 green bell pepper, seeded and diced
- 1 yellow onion, peeled and minced
- Sriracha – 1 tablespoon
- 6 scallions, chopped
- 1 beaten egg
- Zest and juice of 1 medium lime
- Soy sauce – 1 teaspoon
- Mayonnaise – ¼ cup
- Olive oil, for frying

THE SMOKE

- Load smoker with alder briquettes and preheat to 140°F (60°C).

METHOD

1. First, prepare the marinade. Combine the salt, sugar, water, and soy sauce in a large bowl.
2. Slice the tuna into 3-ins (7.5-cm) pieces and place in the marinade. Chill for half an hour.
3. Place the tuna in the smoker and smoke for an hour. When done, take the fish out of the smoker and use a fork to flake it. Add the flaked tuna to a large bowl along with the celery, breadcrumbs, bell pepper, onion, sriracha, scallions, beaten egg, lime zest and juice, soy sauce, and mayonnaise. Using clean hands, combine. Form the mixture into small, equally-sized patties.
4. Add olive oil to a skillet over moderate heat. When the oil is piping hot, add the patties and shallow fry for 5 minutes each side until golden.
5. Serve straight away.

SMOKEY TUNA TACOS

(TOTAL COOK TIME 2 HOURS)

INGREDIENTS FOR 6 SERVINGS

THE FISH

- Ahi tuna (1-lb, 0.5-kg)
- Brown sugar – ½ cup
- Sea salt – ¼ cup

THE SOPES

- Masa cor flour – 2 cups
- Water – 1¼ cups
- Salt – ¼ teaspoon

THE TOMATILLO SAUCE

- Tomatillos, husked – 1 cup
- 1 onion, peeled, halved, and divided
- 2 jalapeno peppers, divided
- A pinch of salt, to season

THE PICO DE GALLO

- 4 tomatoes, diced
- 2 avocados, peeled, pitted, and diced
- A bunch of fresh cilantro, chopped
- Freshly squeezed juice for 3 limes
- ½ head cabbage, shredded
- Queso fresco, crumbled (6-oz, 170-gm)

THE SMOKE

- Preheat your smoker to 225°F (110°C)

METHOD

1. Place the tuna on a chopping board.
2. In a bowl, combine the brown sugar with ¼ cup salt.
3. Score the skin of the tuna with a sharp knife. Then, rub the brown sugar and salt mixture into the scores.
4. Smoke the fish for around 60 minutes, or until its internal temperature registers 140-155°F (60-70°C).
5. In a second bowl for the sopes, combine the cornflour with the water to create a slightly sticky dough. Evenly divide the dough into large balls.
6. Using your hands, flatten the dough balls to a 0.25-in (0.6-cm) thickness.

CONTINUED

7. Cook for 3-4 minutes, on each side until golden brown. Allow the sopes to cool on a wire baking rack.
8. Preheat a grill for moderately high heat, and lightly oil the grate.
9. For the sauce. Place the tomatillos, ½ onion, and 1 jalapeno pepper on the grill. Cook for around 5 minutes until charred on all sides. Transfer the mixture to a food blender, process to a sauce, and season with salt.
10. For the pico de gallo. Dice the remaining onion and jalapeno pepper and combine with tomatoes, avocado, and cilantro in a bowl. Season the mixture with fresh lime juice and season with salt.
11. Transfer the sopes to serving plates, and top with smoked tuna, tomatillo sauce, and avocado mixture.
12. Garnish with cabbage and crumbled cheese, and enjoy.

TUNA STEAKS

(TOTAL COOK TIME 1 HOUR 10 MINUTES)

INGREDIENTS FOR 6 SERVINGS

THE FISH

- 6 tuna steaks

THE MARINADE

- Water - 3 cups
- Kosher salt – ¼ cup
- Brown sugar - ⅓ cup
- Reduced-sodium soy sauce – ¼ cup
- Freshly squeezed juice of 2 limes
- A thumb size piece of ginger, peeled and crushed

THE SMOKE

- Set the smoker to 200°F (90°C)
- Choose your favorite flavor of wood chips

METHOD

1. Add the water, salt, sugar, soy sauce, fresh lime juice, and ginger to a big bowl, and mix well to combine to dissolve the salt and sugar.
2. Add the tuna to ziplock bag, and then pour in the marinade. Transfer the bag to the fridge for 3 hours.
3. Remove the fish from the bag, and rinse under cold running water. Using a kitchen paper towel, pat dry.
4. Lay the fish directly on the smoker's grates and smoke for around 90 minutes or until the fish registers an internal temperature of 140°F (60 °C).
5. Remove the tuna steaks from the smoker and enjoy.

CITRUS MARINATED SCALLOPS

CHAPTER 4

SEAFOOD

BACON-WRAPPED SHRIMP AND CRAB BITES 48
CITRUS MARINATED SCALLOPS 49
CREAMY SMOKED OYSTER SPREAD 51
GARLIC BUTTER LOBSTER TAILS 52
PECAN SMOKED SHRIMP WITH BOOZY BBQ SAUCE 54
KING CRAB LEGS IN LEMON BUTTER 55
LITTLENECK SMOKED CLAMS 56
SHRIMP COCKTAIL 58
SMOKED WHITE WINE MUSSELS 59

BACON-WRAPPED SHRIMP AND CRAB BITES
(TOTAL COOK TIME 45 MINUTES)

INGREDIENTS FOR 4 SERVINGS

THE SEAFOOD

- 25 shrimp, peeled and veined
- Thin-cut rashers of bacon, sliced in half (2-lb, 0.9-kgs)

THE SEASONING

- Cayenne pepper – ½ teaspoon
- Paprika – 2 teaspoons
- Salt – ½ teaspoon
- Black pepper – ½ teaspoon

THE CRAB

- Crab meat – ½ cup
- Cream cheese – 1 cup

THE SMOKE

- Half an hour before you are ready to begin smoking, load your smoked you're your choice of wood chips and preheat to moderately high heat.

METHOD

1. Combine the cayenne pepper, paprika, salt, and black pepper in a small bowl.
2. Arrange the shrimp on a flat plate and season them on both sides with the pepper/paprika mixture.
3. In a second bowl, combine the crab meat and cream cheese and spoon a little of the mixture on top of each shrimp.
4. In a skillet over moderate heat, fry the bacon until half cooked. Take out of the skillet and arrange on paper towel-lined plates to soak up any excess grease.
5. Wrap a piece of bacon around each shrimp and secure using a toothpick.
6. Place the bacon-wrapped shrimp on the smoker and cook for just over half an hour until the shrimp is cooked through and the bacon is just crispy.
7. Serve straight away.

CITRUS MARINATED SCALLOPS
(TOTAL COOK TIME 1 HOUR)

INGREDIENTS FOR 4 SERVINGS

THE SEAFOOD
- Diver scallops (1-lb, 0.5-kgs)

THE MARINADE
- Sugar – ½ teaspoon
- Kosher salt – 1 teaspoon
- Zest of 3 limes
- Fish sauce – ¼ cup

THE SMOKE
- Load grill with water-soaked cherry/apple wood chips and preheat to 350°F (180°C).

METHOD

1. First, make the marinade. Combine the sugar, salt, lime zest, and fish sauce in a large bowl.
2. Add the scallops to the bowl and gently toss to coat. Cover the bowl tightly with kitchen wrap and chill for half an hour.
3. Place the scallops in the smoker and cook for just over 15 minutes until their internal temperature registers 140°F (60°C).
4. Serve straight away.

GARLIC BUTTER LOBSTER TAILS

CREAMY SMOKED OYSTER SPREAD

(TOTAL COOK TIME 1 HOUR 15 MINUTES)

INGREDIENTS FOR 6-8 SERVINGS

THE SEAFOOD

- Fresh oysters in their liquor – 2 cups

THE DIP

- Mayonnaise – 1 cup
- Cream cheese, at room temperature (16-oz, 450-gms)
- Fresh lemon juice – 1 tablespoon
- Old Bay seasoning – 1 tablespoon
- Horseradish – 1 tablespoon
- Hot sauce – 1 tablespoon
- Dijon mustard – 1 tablespoon
- Fresh parsley, chopped (2 tablespoons)
- 1 shallot (grated)
- Scallions, chopped (2 tablespoons)

THE SMOKE

- Using water-smoked wood chips, preheat charcoal in one corner of the smoker and burn until the embers glow then add the wood chips. Allow to burn until the flames die down. The grill should be approximately 200°F (95°C).

METHOD

1. Add the fresh oysters and their juice to a skillet. Arrange the skillet on the smoker grill on the opposite side of the hot charcoals.
2. Close the lid of the smoker and cook for an hour.
3. In the meantime, add the remaining dip ingredients (the mayonnaise, cream cheese, lemon juice, Old Bay seasoning, horseradish, hot sauce, mustard, parsley shallot, scallions) to a bowl and stir until fluffy.
4. Fold the smoked oysters into the dip and serve straight away.

GARLIC BUTTER LOBSTER TAILS
(TOTAL COOK TIME 30 MINUTES)

INGREDIENTS FOR 6 SERVINGS

THE SEAFOOD
- 6 lobster tails

THE GARLIC BUTTER
- 4 garlic cloves (peeled)
- Salted butter – ¼ cup

THE SMOKE
- Preheat smoker to 400°F (210°C).

METHOD

1. Using kitchen scissors, cut open the lobster tails. Slide a knife around the edge of the shells to release the meat, but do not remove it from the shell.
2. Next, make the garlic butter. In a saucepan over moderately low heat, melt together the butter and garlic.
3. Drizzle the melted butter over the prepared lobster tails.
4. Place the lobster on the grill and smoked until the meat registers an internal temperature of 140°F (60°C).
5. Take the lobster tails off the heat and allow them to rest at room temperature for 5 minutes.
6. Use a fork to carefully remove the meat from the shells. Transfer the meat to a serving plate. Drizzle with any leftover garlic butter and serve straight away.

KING CRAB LEGS IN LEMON BUTTER

PECAN SMOKED SHRIMP WITH BOOZY BBQ SAUCE

(TOTAL COOK TIME 1 HOUR 20 MINS)

INGREDIENTS FOR 4-8 SERVINGS

THE SEAFOOD

- Shrimp, peeled and deveined, rinsed, drained, and patted dry. Total weight (2-lb, 0.9-kg)
- Cajun seasoning – 3 tablespoons
- Extra-virgin olive oil – 1 tablespoon

THE SAUCE

- Butter, divided – 6 tablespoons
- 4 scallions, trimmed, white and green parts, thinly sliced crosswise. Separate the white parts from the greens
- Bourbon – ¼ cup
- Beer – ¼ cup
- Louisiana hot sauce – 1 tablespoon
- Worcestershire sauce – 3 tablespoons
- Freshly squeezed lemon juice – 1 tablespoon
- Brown sugar – 1 tablespoon
- Heavy whipping cream - ⅓ cup
- Sea salt and black pepper to season

THE SMOKE

- Preheat the smoker with the lid closed to 250°F (120°C). Pecan wood chips are a good choice for this recipe

METHOD

1. In a bowl, combine the shrimp with Cajun seasoning, and stir to incorporate. Next, stir through the olive oil.
2. Lightly oil a mesh grilling basket or grate. Place the shrimp in a single layer and transfer to the smoker. Smoke the shrimp until firm and smoke-bronzed for 30-45 minutes.
3. In the meantime, prepare the sauce. In a frying pan, melt 3 tablespoons of butter over moderately high heat. Set aside 2 tablespoons of the green parts of the scallions. Add the remaining scallions to the frying pan, and sauté, stirring with a wooden spoon, for 3 minutes, until beginning to brown.

CONTINUED

4. Pour in the bourbon and beer, and boil until the mixture is reduced by around half. Then, add hot sauce, Worcestershire sauce, lemon juice, and brown sugar and boil for 60 seconds. Finally, add the whipping cream along with the remaining butter and hot sauce and boil until thickened, for 5 minutes.
5. Season the sauce with salt and pepper, and sweeten with more sugar if needed. The sauce will need to be heavily seasoned.
6. Transfer the shrimp from the smoker to the pan with the sauce. Scatter over the green parts of the scallions set aside earlier.
7. Enjoy.

KING CRAB LEGS IN LEMON BUTTER
(TOTAL COOK TIME 45 MINUTES)

INGREDIENTS FOR 4 SERVINGS

THE SEAFOOD
- King crab legs (6-lb, 2.7-kgs)

THE BUTTER
- Salted butter – 1 cup
- Fresh minced garlic – 2 tablespoons
- Lemon pepper seasoning – 2 tablespoons
- Fresh lemon juice – ¼ cup

THE SMOKE
- Load your smoker grill with wood chips and preheat to 225°F (110°C).

METHOD
1. First, prepare the lemon butter. Combine the butter, garlic, lemon pepper seasoning, and lemon juice in a bowl. Melt the mixture using a microwave oven.
2. Place the crab legs on the smoker and cook for just under half an hour, basting with lemon butter every 10 minutes.
3. After 25 minutes, move the legs to the hottest part of the smoker for 5 minutes. Flip the legs after 2½ minutes. The crab legs should have light grill marks. Serve straight away.

LITTLENECK SMOKED CLAMS
(TOTAL COOK TIME 1 HOUR 45 MINUTES)

INGREDIENTS FOR 4 SERVINGS

THE SEAFOOD

- Littleneck clams (3-lb, 1.5-kgs)
- Small handful fresh parsley, chopped
- Lemon wedges, to serve

THE SMOKE

- Load your smoker grill with maple/apple wood and preheat to 225°F (110°C).

METHOD

1. Clean the clams by soaking them in water for 60 minutes then scrubbing them with a brush under running water.
2. Shuck the clams using a clam knife. You should be left with each of the clams resting in just one half of the shell.
3. Place the clams on the smoker and cook for approximately half an hour. You may need to use a dehydrator grate to prevent the clams from falling through the grills.
4. Garnish with parsley and serve straight away with fresh lemon wedges.

SMOKED WHITE WINE MUSSELS

SHRIMP COCKTAIL
(TOTAL COOK TIME 45 MINUTES)

INGREDIENTS FOR 4 SERVINGS

THE SEAFOOD

- Brown shrimp, peeled and veined (1-lb, 0.5-kgs)

THE COCKTAIL

- Kosher salt – 1 teaspoon
- Cumin – 1 tablespoon
- Fresh parsley, roughly chopped – ¼ cup
- Fresh lemon juice – 2 tablespoon
- Cocktail sauce – 1 cup

THE SMOKE

- Preheat the smoker grill to 200°F (95°C).

METHOD

1. Combine the salt, cumin, parsley, and lemon juice in a large bowl. Add the shrimp and toss to coat in the mixture.
2. Arrange the seasoned shrimp on the smoker and cook for just over 20 minutes until the shrimp curl and become a pale pink.
3. Take the shrimp out of the smoker, allow to cool to room temperature, then chill until cold through.
4. Toss the cold shrimp in the cocktail sauce and serve.

SMOKED WHITE WINE MUSSELS
(TOTAL COOK TIME 2 HOURS 30 MINUTES)

INGREDIENTS FOR 4 SERVINGS

THE SEAFOOD

- Mussels, debearded (4-lb, 1.8-kgs)

THE MARINADE

- Water – 1 cup
- White wine – 1 cup
- Walnut oil – ¼ cup

THE SMOKE

- Using cherry/apple wood, preheat the smoker to 145°F (65°C).

METHOD

1. In a large pot, over moderately high heat, bring the water and white wine to a boil.
2. Working in batches, arrange a single layer of mussels in the pot, cover with a lid and steam for a few minutes until the shells open. Discard any unopened shells. Repeat until all mussels have been steamed.
3. Strain the cooking liquid through cheesecloth and set to one side to use later.
4. Remove the mussels from the shells using a toothpick and drop into the set-aside broth. Allow the mussels to soak at room temperature for half an hour.
5. Arrange the mussels in the smoker and smoke for 1½-2 hours. You may need to use a dehydrator grate to prevent the mussels from falling through the grates.
6. Toss the smoked mussels in walnut oil and serve straight away.

CAJUN SMOKED CATFISH

CHAPTER 5

MORE FISH

APPLE SMOKED TILAPIA WITH GINGER AND GRAPEFRUIT MARINADE 62
CAJUN SMOKED CATFISH 63
HOISIN AND ORANGE SMOKED TILAPIA 65
HONEY LIME SMOKED SNAPPER 66
HOT SMOKED KINGFISH 67
MAHI MAHI WITH CORN AND WATERMELON SALAD 69
MAPLE SMOKED SMELT 71
SMOKED CATFISH WITH A HERB MARINADE 72
SMOKED HALIBUT IN A TANGERINE AND HOISIN SAUCE GLAZE 74
SWORDFISH IN LEMON AND OLIVE OIL 75

APPLE SMOKED TILAPIA WITH GINGER AND GRAPEFRUIT MARINADE

(TOTAL COOK TIME 1 HOUR 15 MINUTES)

INGREDIENTS FOR 6-8 SERVINGS

THE FISH

- 4 tilapia fillets

THE MARINADE

- 2 large grapefruits, peeled and sliced into quarters
- 3 cloves garlic, peeled
- A thumb of ginger root, peeled, cut into small chunks
- Vegetable oil – ¼ cup
- Brown sugar – 1 cup
- Fish sauce – 2 tablespoons
- Sea salt – ½ teaspoon

THE SMOKE

- Load the smoker with applewood chips and preheat to 275°F (135°C).

METHOD

1. First, prepare the marinade. In a food blender, combine the grapefruit along with the garlic, ginger, oil, brown sugar, fish sauce, and salt and process until silky smooth and fully incorporated.
2. Place the fish in a shallow dish and cover with the marinade, turning until evenly coated.
3. Cover the dish with kitchen wrap and transfer to the fridge for approximately 2 hours.
4. Remove the fillets from the marinade, gently shaking off any excess marinade and arrange the fish fillets on a smoking rack.
5. Smoke for 2 hours, until the fish reaches an internal temperature of 145°F (65°C).
6. Serve and enjoy.

CAJUN SMOKED CATFISH

(TOTAL COOK TIME 7 HOURS)

INGREDIENTS FOR 6 SERVINGS

THE FISH

- 6 catfish fillets

THE BRINE

- Room temperature water
- Salt – 1 cup

SEASONING

- Louisiana hot sauce – 1 cup
- Cajun seasoning – to taste
- Sea salt and coarsely ground black pepper

THE SMOKE

- Preheat a smoker to 200°F (95°C). Add the apple wood or cherry chips.

METHOD

1. To help prevent the fish from drying out, first brine the fillets. To do this, fill two casserole dishes 50 percent full with room temperature water. Add ½ cup of salt to each of the dishes. Lay the fish fillets inside the salted water. Transfer the casserole dish to the fridge to brine, for no less than 4 hours.
2. Remove the fish from the fridge and using kitchen paper towel, pat dry.
3. Drizzle with hot sauce and season well with Cajun seasoning, salt, and ground black pepper.
4. Lay the fish fillets on the smoker grate and close the smoker lid, positioning the vents between ½-¾ open. Adjust the vents as necessary to ensure that a constant temperature is achieved during the smoking process.
5. Smoke for between 2-2½ hours until the fish flakes easily when using a fork and the middle of the fish is warmed through.
6. Remove the fish from the smoker and while covered, loosely tent with aluminum foil, allow to rest for 15 minutes.
7. Serve and enjoy.

HOISIN AND ORANGE SMOKED TILAPIA

HOISIN AND ORANGE SMOKED TILAPIA
(TOTAL COOK TIME 4 HOURS 5 MINUTES)

INGREDIENTS FOR 4 SERVINGS

THE FISH
- 4 tilapia fillets

THE MARINADE
- Freshly squeezed orange juice – 1 cup
- Hoisin sauce – 1 cup
- Sriracha sauce – 1 tablespoon
- Salt – 2 teaspoons

THE SMOKE
- Preheat a smoker to 275°F (135°C) using apple or alder wood chips

METHOD

1. First, make the marinade. In a bowl, combine the fresh orange juice with the hoisin sauce followed by the Sriracha and salt, and stir until the hoisin sauce is entirely dissolved.
2. Add the fish to a large mixing bowl and pour the marinade evenly over the fish, turning the tilapia until evenly coated. Cover the bowl with kitchen wrap and transfer to the fridge to chill for approximately 2 hours.
3. Remove the fish from the marinade, gently shaking off any excess marinade and lay the fillets on the smoker rack.
4. Smoke the tilapia until they reach an internal temperature of 145°F (65°C); for approximately 2 hours.
5. Serve the fish warm.

HONEY LIME SMOKED SNAPPER
(TOTAL COOK TIME 1 HOUR 15 MINUTES)

INGREDIENTS FOR 4-6 SERVINGS

THE FISH

- Snapper fillets, skinless, boneless, trimmed of red (1 ½ -lb, 0.80kgs each)

THE MARINADE

- Honey – ¼ cup
- Sea salt – ¼ cup
- Cracked black peppercorns – 1 tablespoon
- Cloves – 2 whole
- 2 allspice berries
- Zest of 1 lime, removed in strips

THE SMOKE

- Set the smoker according to the manufacturer's directions and preheat to 275° F (135°C). Add alder wood chips.

METHOD

1. In a large bowl, combine the honey along with the salt, cracked black peppercorns, cloves, and allspice berries. Add sufficient water to cover, and whisk thoroughly, until the salt and honey are entirely dissolved. Stir in the lime zest to combine.
2. Add the fish to the bowl, and cover with kitchen wrap.
3. Transfer to the fridge for no less 12 hours, flipping over several times.
4. Drain the snapper, and discard the brine along with the zest.
5. Under cold running tap water, thoroughly rinse the fish and pat totally dry with kitchen paper towel.
6. Lay the fish on an oiled wire rack and set over a rimmed baking sheet.
7. Allow the fish to air-dry in the fridge until the surface is slightly tacky; this will take around 2 hours.
8. Smoke the snapper on the wire rack until bronzed all over and totally cooked through; for between 30-46 minutes.

CONTINUED

9. The fish is ready when it flakes easily when using a fork and it reaches an internal temperature in its thickest part of 140°F (60°C).
10. Transfer the fish to a rack set over a rimmed baking sheet to cool. When at room temperature, wrap in kitchen wrap and transfer to the fridge until you are ready to serve.
11. The fish will keep for up to 72 hours in the fridge.

HOT SMOKED KINGFISH
(TOTAL COOK TIME 1 HOUR 5 MINUTES)

INGREDIENTS FOR 4 SERVINGS

THE FISH
- Yellowtail kingfish fillets, skin on (2-lb, 0.90-kgs)
- Olive oil cooking spray

THE BRINE
- Salt (14-oz, 0.4-kgs)
- Dark brown sugar (0.7-oz, 0.20-kgs)
- Water – 8 cups

THE SMOKE
- Using a portable smoker, fill the burners half-full with methylated spirits and light.
- Spread a heaped tablespoon of oak wood chips to the smoker pan.
- Play the tray above the wood.
- Oil the rack using olive oil spray and arrange over the top of the tray.

METHOD
1. First, make the brine by mixing the salt with the sugar and water in a large container.
2. Add the fish to the brine and set to one side for 30 minutes.
3. Wash the brine off the kingfish fillet and pat dry with kitchen paper towel.
4. Lay the fillets on the rack, skin side facing downwards. Cover, and with the ventilator open, smoke for between 45-50 minutes.
5. The fish is ready to serve when the thickest part reaches an internal temperature of 140°F (60°C).
6. Serve.

MAHI MAHI WITH CORN AND WATERMELON SALAD

MAHI MAHI WITH CORN AND WATERMELON SALAD
(TOTAL COOK TIME 35 MINUTES)

INGREDIENTS FOR 2-4 SERVINGS

THE FISH

- 4 mahi-mahi fillets (6-oz, 0.20-kgs each)

THE INGREDIENTS

- 2 ears of corn
- Olive oil – 2 tablespoons
- Salt – ½ tablespoon
- Black pepper – 1 teaspoon
- Watermelon, cut into bite-sized cubes – 3 cups
- Feta cheese, crumbled – ¼ cup
- Olive oil – 3 tablespoons
- 1 fresh lime
- Sea salt

THE SMOKE

- When you ready to cook, and with the lid open, start the grill on smoke until the fire is established, for between 4-5 minutes.
- Set the temperature to 350°F (180°C) and with the lid closed, preheat for between 10-15 minutes.

METHOD

1. Lay the corn directly on the grill grate and cook for 20-25 minutes, until the corn kernels are bite tender and sufficiently cooked through.
2. Remove the corn from the grill and allow the corn to come to room temperature.
3. Next, adjust the grill temperature heat to high and with the lid closed, preheat for between 10-15 minutes.
4. Lightly brush the fish with oil and season with salt and black pepper.
5. Lay the fish directly on the hot grill and smoke until the thickest part of the fish registers an internal temperature of 145°F (65°C).
6. In the meantime, and while the fish smokes prepare the watermelon salad. Slice the kernels off the cob over a bowl. Add the cubes of watermelon and crumbled feta to the corn. Drizzle with oil and fresh lime juice and season to taste.
7. When you are ready to serve, arrange the salad on a platter and lay the fish on top.

MAPLE SMOKED SMELT

MAPLE SMOKED SMELT

(TOTAL COOK TIME 4 HOURS 15 MINUTES)

INGREDIENTS FOR 4-6 SERVINGS

THE FISH

- Smelt, cleaned (1 -lb, 0.5-kgs)

THE MARINADE

- Cold water – 2 cups
- Freshly squeezed apple juice – 2 cups
- Brown sugar – ¼ cup
- Soy sauce – 2 tablespoons
- Garlic powder – 1 tablespoon
- Freshly ground black pepper – 1 tablespoon
- Paprika – 1 tablespoon
- Cayenne pepper – 1 teaspoon

THE SMOKE

- Set the smoker to 200° F (95°C). Add maple wood chips.

METHOD

1. In a bowl, combine the water with the freshly squeezed apple juice, brown sugar, soy sauce, garlic powder, black pepper, paprika, and cayenne pepper, and stir to dissolve.
2. Lay the smelt in a flat dish and add the marinade. Stir well and using kitchen wrap, cover. Transfer to the fridge to marinate for between 4-6 hours.
3. Rinse the fish under cold running tap water, pat dry with kitchen paper towel and lay on a smoker rack.
4. Place the fish in a dry and cool place for between 35-45 minutes, until a pellicle* form on the surface of the smelt.
5. Smoke the fish for 3-4 hours, or until the thickest part of the smelt registers an internal temperature reaches 145°F (65°C)
6. Serve hot.

*A pellicle is a coating or skin of protein which naturally forms on the surface of fish/meat/poultry. It allows smoke to adhere to the surface of the fish better during the smoking process for a more intense and full-bodied flavor.

SMOKED CATFISH WITH A HERB MARINADE

(TOTAL COOK TIME 3 HOURS 35 MINUTES)

INGREDIENTS FOR 4 SERVINGS

THE FISH

- 4 catfish fillets

THE MARINADE

- Olive oil – 1 cup
- Red wine vinegar – ½ cup
- Juice of 1 fresh lemon
- 1 clove garlic, peeled, minced
- Thyme – 1 tablespoon
- Basil – 1 tablespoon
- Black pepper – 1 teaspoon
- Cayenne pepper – 1 teaspoon
- Salt – 1 tablespoon
- Sugar – 3 tablespoons

THE SMOKE

- Set the smoker to 225° F (110°C). Add alder wood chips

METHOD

1. In a bowl, make the marinade by combining the oil with the red wine vinegar, along with the fresh lemon juice, garlic, thyme, basil, pepper, cayenne pepper, salt, and sugar. Mix to incorporate.
2. Pour the marinade over the fish fillets, turning them to make sure they are evenly and well coated.
3. Cover the bowl with kitchen wrap and transfer to the fridge for 60 minutes.
4. Lay the fish on racks and place in the smoker.
5. Smoke for 2 hours 20 minutes until the fish flakes easily when using a fork and is cooked through.
6. Serve.

SWORDFISH IN LEMON AND OLIVE OIL

SMOKED HALIBUT IN A TANGERINE AND HOISIN SAUCE GLAZE
(TOTAL COOK TIME 4 HOURS 10 MINUTES)

INGREDIENTS FOR 2-3 SERVINGS

THE FISH

- 1 halibut fillet (2-lb, 0.9-kgs)

THE MARINADE

- Hoisin sauce – ½ cup
- Freshly squeezed tangerine juice – ⅔ cup
- Runny honey – ½ cup
- Sriracha sauce – 1½ tablespoons
- Sesame oil – 2 tablespoons
- Garlic powder – 1 teaspoon
- Toasted sesame seeds, to serve– 1 tablespoon

THE SMOKE

- Preheat a smoker to 250°F (120°C) using alder wood chips.

METHOD

1. First, make the marinade. In a bowl, combine the hoisin sauce with the fresh tangerine juice, runny honey, Sriracha sauce, sesame oil, and garlic powder, and mixing well to combine. Measure out ½ cup of the marinade and put to one side.
2. Lay the salmon in a single layer, in a flat dish. Pour the remaining marinade over the fish, making sure it is evenly and well coated. Cover the dish with kitchen wrap and transfer to the fridge for between 3-4 hours. Flip the fish over every 60 minutes.
3. Smoke the salmon for approximately 3 hours, until the internal temperature of the salmon reaches 145°F (65°C).
4. While the fish smokes, pour the marinade set aside earlier into a small pan and bring to a low boil to reduce and thicken to form a glaze, for 8-10 minutes. Remove the pan from the heat.
5. When the salmon is sufficiently cooked through, transfer it to a serving platter.
6. Brush the salmon all over with the glaze and garnish with toasted sesame seeds.
7. Serve and enjoy.

SWORDFISH IN LEMON AND OLIVE OIL
(TOTAL COOK TIME 30 MINUTES)

INGREDIENTS FOR 4-8 SERVINGS

THE FISH

- 4 swordfish fillets (0.5 -lb, 250-gms each)

THE INGREDIENTS

- Virgin olive oil – ½ cup + 2 tablespoons
- Freshly squeezed juice of 1 lemon
- Hot water – 2 tablespoons
- 2 garlic cloves, peeled, minced
- Fresh parsley, chopped – 3 tablespoons
- Fresh oregano, finely chopped – 1 tablespoon
- Brined capers, drained – 1 tablespoon
- Salt and black pepper, to season

THE SMOKE

- Alder wood chips are ideal for this recipe.
- With the lid open, start the grill on smoke and establish the fire, this will take between 4-5 minutes.
- Preheat the temperature to 400°F (210°C), with the lid closed for between 10-15 minutes.

METHOD

1. Add ½ cup of oil to a pan and over low heat, warm the olive oil.
2. Whisk in the fresh lemon juice followed by the hot water.
3. Stir in the garlic along with the parsley, oregano, and capers. Season with a pinch of salt and a dash of pepper.
4. Brush the swordfish with the remaining 2 tablespoons of oil and season.
5. Lay the fish on the grill grate and smoke until the fish flakes easily when using a fork, for 15-20 minutes. Timings will depend on whether you prefer the fish cooked medium or rare.
6. Transfer to a serving platter and drizzle with the warm oil sauce.

SPICY PINK GRAPEFRUIT AND HERB MARINADE FOR FISH

CHAPTER 6

SAUCES

LEMON AND DILL SALMON SEASONING 78
HONEY LIME MARINADE FOR SALMON 79
LEMON BUTTER SAUCE 81
SPICY PINK GRAPEFRUIT AND HERB MARINADE FOR FISH 82
BASTE FOR GRILLED FISH 84
ORANGE-SAGE RUB FOR MEAT, POULTRY, AND FISH 85
SPICY PINK GRAPEFRUIT AND HERB MARINADE FOR FISH 87

LEMON AND DILL SALMON SEASONING

(TOTAL TIME 3 MINUTES)

INGREDIENTS FOR ½ CUP

THE INGREDIENTS

- Olive oil – 4 tablespoons
- Dried dill weed – 2 tablespoons
- Kosher salt – 1 tablespoon
- Freshly ground black pepper – 1 tablespoon
- Garlic powder – 2 teaspoons

METHOD

1. In a bowl, combine the oil with the dill weed, kosher salt, black pepper, and garlic powder.
2. To use: Spread the seasoning on all sides of salmon fillets, excluding the skin, and cook as directed.

HONEY LIME MARINADE FOR SALMON
(TOTAL TIME 1 HOUR)

INGREDIENTS FOR 1 CUP
THE INGREDIENTS

- Pure honey - 5 tablespoons
- Zest of 1 fresh lime
- Freshly squeezed lime juice – 2 tablespoons
- Cornstarch – 1 teaspoon
- Sriracha – 1 teaspoons

METHOD

1. Over moderate heat, in a small pan, combine the honey with the lime zest, lime juice, cornstarch, and Sriracha, until the cornstarch is dissolved entirely. When no bits of gritty cornstarch remain, turn the heat to moderate-high. Continue to whisk and simmer for approximately 60 minutes until thickened.
2. Remove the pan from the heat, cover with a lid and keep the glaze warm. Use as needed.

LEMON BUTTER SAUCE

LEMON BUTTER SAUCE

(TOTAL TIME 5 MINUTES)

INGREDIENTS FOR ⅓ CUP

THE INGREDIENTS

- Unsalted butter, chopped into pieces – ¼ cup
- 1 garlic clove, peeled and grated
- Sea salt – ¼ teaspoon
- Freshly squeezed lemon juice – 2 tablespoons
- Freshly ground black pepper, to season
- Fresh parsley, chopped, to garnish
- A pinch of red pepper flakes, to serve, optional

METHOD

1. Over low heat, and in a small pan, melt the butter.
2. Add the garlic and salt to the pan and cook for 60 seconds.
3. Take the pan off the heat, and add the fresh lemon juice. Season with pepper and sprinkle over the chopped parsley and red pepper flakes.
4. Serve the sauce with fish, over pasta or rice.

SPICY PINK GRAPEFRUIT AND HERB MARINADE FOR FISH

(TOTAL TIME 10 MINUTES)

INGREDIENTS FOR 4 SERVINGS

THE INGREDIENTS

- 1 large pink grapefruit
- Olive oil – ¼ cup
- Honey – 2 tablespoons
- Soy sauce – 3 tablespoons
- Fresh basil, chopped – 1 tablespoon
- Fresh rosemary, chopped – 1 tablespoon
- Red pepper flakes, crushed - ⅛ teaspoon
- 2 garlic cloves, peeled and chopped

METHOD

1. Use a zester to grate 1 teaspoon of zest from the grapefruit and add to a bowl. Cut the grapefruit in half and squeeze the juice from the fruit into the bowl with the zest.
2. To the same bowl, add the oil, honey, soy sauce, basil, rosemary, red pepper flakes, and garlic. Stir to combine and pour over your choice of fish.
3. For best results, allow the marinade to soak for at least an hour.

BASTE FOR GRILLED FISH

BASTE FOR GRILLED FISH

(TOTAL TIME 10 MINUTES)

INGREDIENTS FOR 6 SERVINGS

THE INGREDIENTS

- Butter – ¼ cup
- Brown sugar – ¼ cup
- Powdered garlic – 1 teaspoon
- Fresh lemon juice – 2 tablespoons
- Soy sauce – ½ -1 tablespoon, as needed
- Black pepper – 1 teaspoon
- A pinch of cayenne pepper

METHOD

1. In a small saucepan, combine the butter, brown sugar, garlic, lemon juice, soy sauce (to taste), black pepper, and a pinch of cayenne. Over low heat, cook until the sugar dissolves. Set aside to cool.
2. Use as directed.

ORANGE-SAGE RUB FOR MEAT, POULTRY, AND FISH

(TOTAL TIME 10 MINUTES)

INGREDIENTS FOR 5-6 TABLESPOONS

THE INGREDIENTS

- Orange zest, freshly grated – 1 tablespoon
- 3 garlic cloves, peeled and finely minced
- Fresh sage, finely minced – 1 tablespoon
- Extra-virgin olive oil – 1 tablespoon
- Honey – 1 tablespoon
- Freshly ground black pepper – ¼ teaspoon
- Salt – ¼ teaspoon

METHOD

1. Combine the orange zest, garlic, sage, oil, honey, black pepper, and salt in a bowl.
2. Use as directed.

ORANGE-SAGE RUB FOR MEAT, POULTRY, AND FISH

SPICY PINK GRAPEFRUIT AND HERB MARINADE FOR FISH

(TOTAL TIME 10 MINUTES)

INGREDIENTS FOR 4 SERVINGS

THE INGREDIENTS

- 1 large pink grapefruit
- Olive oil – ¼ cup
- Honey – 2 tablespoons
- Soy sauce – 3 tablespoons
- Fresh basil, chopped – 1 tablespoon
- Fresh rosemary, chopped – 1 tablespoon
- Red pepper flakes, crushed - ⅛ teaspoon
- 2 garlic cloves, peeled and chopped

METHOD

1. Use a zester to grate 1 teaspoon of zest from the grapefruit and add to a bowl. Cut the grapefruit in half and squeeze the juice from the fruit into the bowl with the zest.
2. To the same bowl, add the oil, honey, soy sauce, basil, rosemary, red pepper flakes, and garlic. Stir to combine and pour over your choice of fish.
3. For best results, allow the marinade to soak for at least an hour.

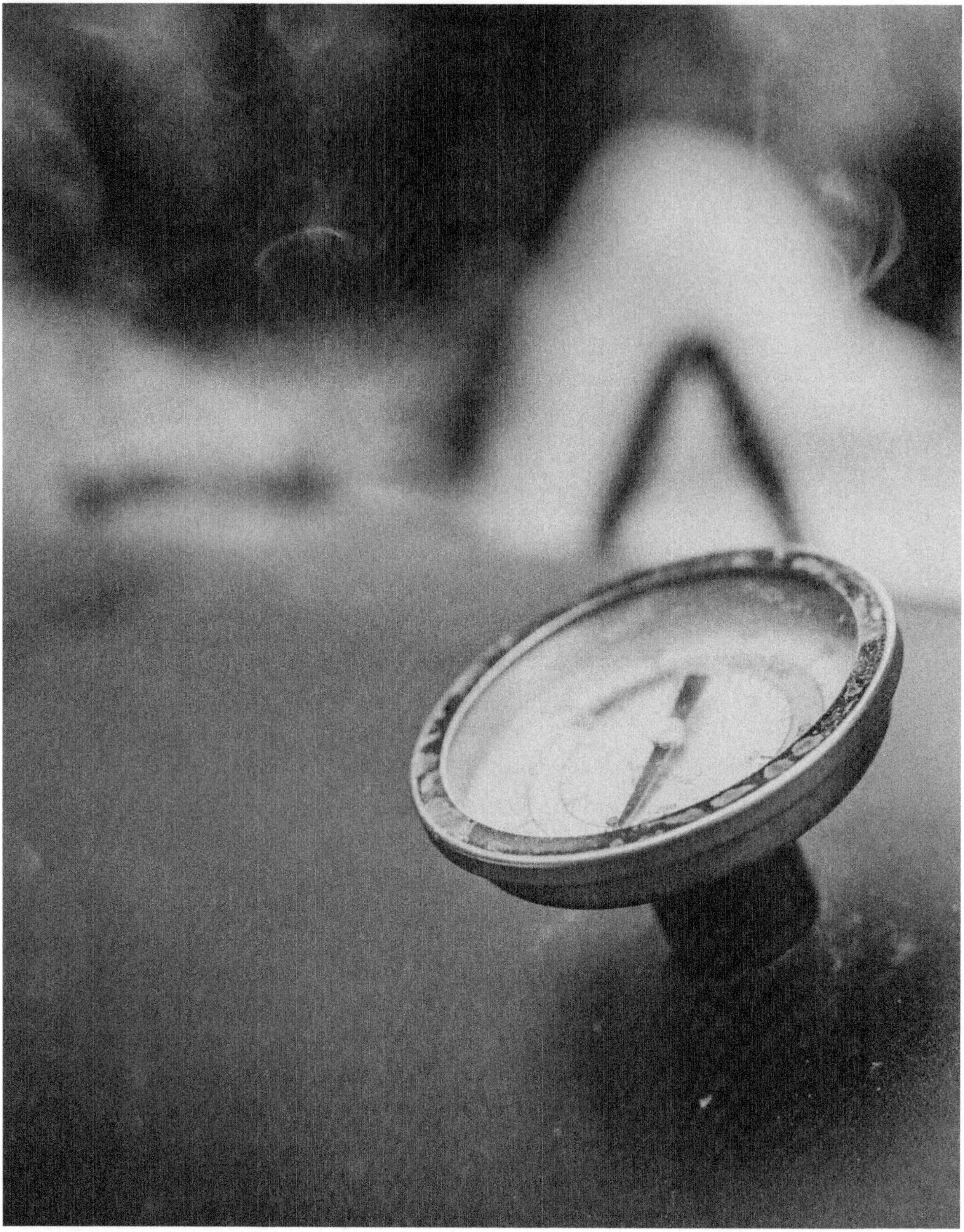

CHAPTER 7

SMOKING MEAT

BARBECUING AND SMOKING MEAT 90
COLD AND HOT SMOKING 91
SELECTING A SMOKER 92
DIFFERENT SMOKER TYPES 93
DIFFERENT SMOKER STYLES 94
CHOOSE YOUR WOOD 95
CHARCOAL 97
RIGHT TEMPERATURE 98
BASIC PREPARATIONS 99
ELEMENTS OF SMOKING 100

BARBECUING AND SMOKING MEAT

You might not believe it, but there are still people who think that the process of Barbequing and Smoking are the same! So, this is something you should know about before diving deeper. So, whenever you use a traditional BBQ grill, you always put your meat directly on top of the heat source for a brief amount of time which eventually cooks up the meal. Smoking, on the other hand, will require you to combine the heat from your grill as well as the smoke to infuse a delicious smoky texture and flavor into your meat. As a result, smoking usually takes much longer than traditional barbecuing. In most cases, it takes a minimum of 2 hours and a temperature of 100 -120 degrees for the smoke to be properly infused into the meat. Keep in mind that the time and temperature will depend on the type of meat you are using, which is why it is suggested to keep a meat thermometer handy to ensure that your meat is doing fine. Also, remember that this barbecuing method is also known as "Low and slow" smoking. With that cleared up, you should be aware that there are two different ways smoking is done.

COLD AND HOT SMOKING

Depending on the type of grill that you are using, you can get the option to go for a Hot Smoking Method or a Cold Smoking One. However, the primary fact about these three different cooking techniques which you should keep in mind are as follows:

- **HOT SMOKING:** In this technique, the food will use both the heat on your grill and the smoke to prepare your food. This method is most suitable for chicken, lamb, brisket, etc.
- **COLD SMOKING:** In this method, you are going to smoke your meat at a very low temperature, such as 85 F (30 degrees Celsius), making sure that it doesn't come into direct contact with the heat. Cold smoking is mainly used
- **ROASTING SMOKE:** This is also known as Smoke Baking. This process is essentially a combined form of roasting and baking and can be performed in any smoker with a capacity to reach temperatures above 180 F (80 degrees Celsius).

SELECTING A SMOKER

You need to invest in a good smoker if you smoke meat regularly. Consider these options when buying a smoker. Here are two natural fire options for you:

- **CHARCOAL SMOKERS:** are fueled by a combination of charcoal and wood. Charcoal burns quickly, and the temperature remains steady so you won't have any problem with a charcoal smoker. The wood gives a great flavor to the meat, and you will enjoy smoking meat.
- **WOOD SMOKER:** The wood smoker will give your brisket and ribs the best smoky flavor and taste, but it is harder to cook with wood. Both hardwood blocks and chips are used as fuel.

DIFFERENT SMOKER TYPES

You should know that in the market, you will get three different types of Smokers

Charcoal Smoker

These smokers are hands down the best for infusing the perfect smoky flavor to your meat. But be warned that these smokers are difficul2t to master as the method of regulating temperature is a little bit difficult compared to standard Gas or Electric smokers.

Electric Smoker

After the charcoal smoker, next comes the more straightforward option, Electric Smokers. These are easy-to-use and plug-and-play types. All you need to do is plug in, set the temperature, and go about your daily life. The smoker will do the rest. However, remember that the smoky finishing flavor won't be as intense as the Charcoal one.

Gas Smokers

Finally, comes the Gas Smokers. These have a reasonably easy temperature control mechanism and are usually powered by LP Gas. The drawback of these Smokers is that you will have to keep checking up on your smoker now and then to ensure that it has enough Gas.

DIFFERENT SMOKER STYLES

The different styles of Smokers are essentially divided into the following.

Vertical (Bullet Style Using Charcoal)

These are usually low-cost solutions and are perfect for first-time smokers.

Vertical (Cabinet Style)

These Smokers have a square-shaped design with cabinets and drawers/trays for easy accessibility. These cookers come with a water tray and a designated wood chips box.

Offset

These types of smokers have dedicated fireboxes that are attached to the side of the main grill. The smoke and heat required for these are generated from the firebox, which is passed through the main chamber and out through a nicely placed chimney.

Kamado Joe

And finally, we have the Kamado Joe, which ceramic smokers are largely regarded as being the "Jack of All Trades." These smokers can be used as low and slow smokers, grills, high or low-temperature ovens, and so on.

They have a thick ceramic wall that allows them to hold heat better than any other smoker, requiring only a little charcoal.

These are easy to use with better insulation and are more efficient when it comes to fuel control.

comes to fuel control.

CHOOSE YOUR WOOD

You need to choose your wood carefully because the type of wood you will use affect significantly to the flavor and taste of the meat. Here are a few options for you:

- **Maple:** Maple has a smoky and sweet taste and goes well with pork or poultry
- **Alder:** Alder is sweet and light. Perfect for poultry and fish.
- **Apple:** Apple has a mild and sweet flavor. Goes well with pork, fish, and poultry.
- **Oak:** Oak is great for slow cooking. Ideal for game, pork, beef, and lamb.
- **Mesquite:** Mesquite has a smoky flavor and is extremely strong. Goes well with pork or beef.
- **Hickory:** Has a smoky and strong flavor. Goes well with beef and lamb.
- **Cherry:** Has a mild and sweet flavor. Great for pork, beef, and turkey

The Different Types Of Wood	Suitable For
Hickory	Wild game, chicken, pork, cheeses, beef
Pecan	Chicken, pork, lamb, cheeses, fish.
Mesquite	Beef and vegetables
Alder	Swordfish, Salmon, Sturgeon and other types of fishes. Works well with pork and chicken too.
Oak	Beef or briskets
Maple	Vegetable, ham or poultry
Cherry	Game birds, poultry or pork
Apple	Game birds, poultry, beef
Peach	Game birds, poultry or pork
Grape Vines	Beef, chicken or turkey
Wine Barrel Chips	Turkey, beef, chicken or cheeses
Seaweed	Lobster, mussels, crab, shrimp etc.
Herbs or Spices such as rosemary, bay leaves, mint, lemon peels, whole nutmeg etc.	Good for cheeses or vegetables and a small collection of light meats such as fillets or fish steaks.

CHARCOAL

In General, there are three different types of charcoal. All of them are porous residues of black color made of carbon and ashes. However, the following are a little distinguishable due to their specific features.

- **BBQ Briquettes:** These are the ones that are made from a fine blend of charcoal and char.
- **Charcoal Briquettes:** These are created by compressing charcoal and are made from sawdust or wood products.
- **Lump Charcoal:** These are made directly from hardwood and are the most premium quality charcoals. They are entirely natural and are free from any form of additives.

RIGHT TEMPERATURE

- Start at 250F (120C): Start your smoker a bit hot. This extra heat gets the smoking process going.

- Temperature drop: Once you add the meat to the smoker, the temperature will drop, which is fine.

- Maintain the temperature. Monitor and maintain the temperature. Keep the temperature steady during the smoking process.

Avoid peeking now and then. Smoke and heat are the two crucial elements that make your meat taste great. If you open the cover every now, and then you lose both of them, and your meat loses flavor. Only open the lid only when you truly need it.

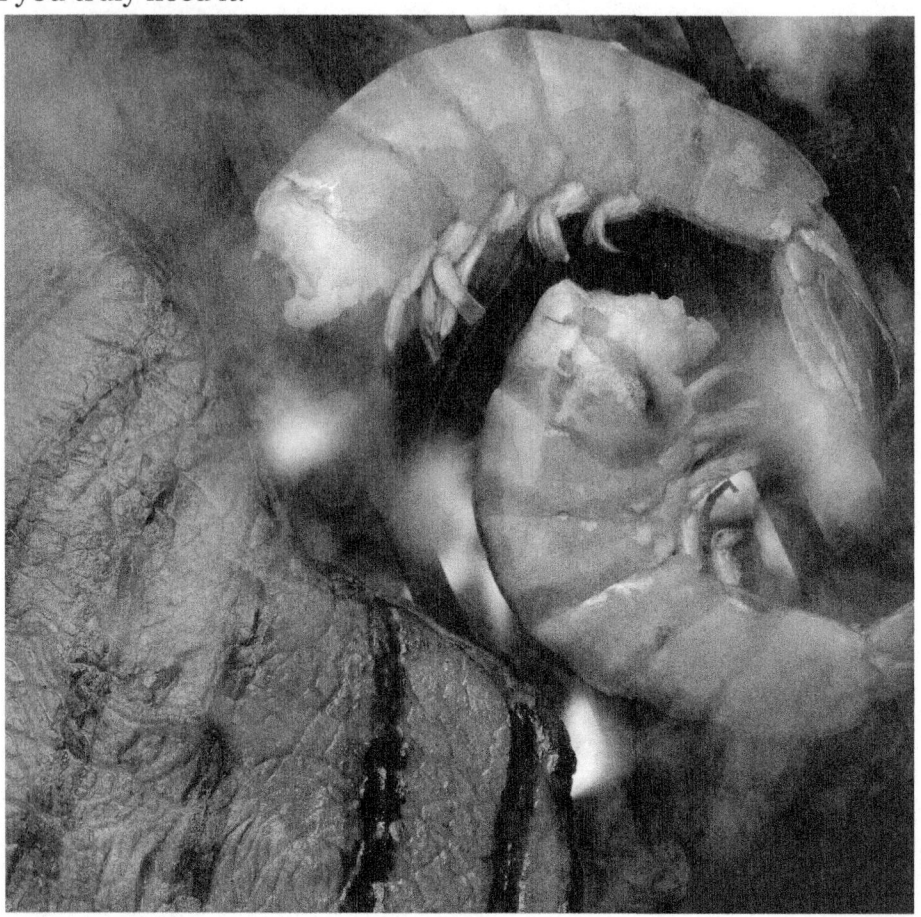

BASIC PREPARATIONS

- Always be prepared to spend the whole day and take as much time as possible to smoke your meat for maximum effect.
- Ensure you obtain the perfect Ribs/Meat for the meal you are trying to smoke. Do a little bit of research if you need.
- I have already added a list of woods. Consult that list and choose the perfect wood for your meal.
- Make sure to prepare the marinade for each of the meals properly. A great deal of the flavors comes from the rubbing.
- Keep a meat thermometer handy to get the internal temperature when needed.
- Use mittens or tongs to keep yourself safe.
- Please refrain from using charcoal infused alongside starter fluid, as it might bring a very unpleasant odor to your food.
- Always start with a small amount of wood and keep adding them as you cook.
- Don't be afraid to experiment with different types of wood for newer flavors and experiences.
- Always keep a notebook near you and note jot down whatever you are doing or learning and use them during future sessions. A notebook will help you to evolve and move forward.

ELEMENTS OF SMOKING

Smoking is a very indirect method of cooking that relies on many factors to give you the most perfectly cooked meal you are looking for. Each component is essential to the whole process as they all work together to create the meal of your dreams.

- **TIME:** Unlike grilling or even Barbequing, smoking takes a long time and requires a lot of patience. It takes time for the smoky flavor to get infused into the meats slowly. Just to compare things, it takes about 8 minutes to thoroughly cook a steak through direct heating, while smoking (indirect heating) will take around 35-40 minutes.
- **TEMPERATURE:** When it comes to smoking, the temperature is affected by many factors that are not only limited to the wind and cold air temperatures but also the cooking wood's dryness. Some smokers work best with large fires that are controlled by the draw of a chimney and restricted airflow through the various vents of the cooking chamber and firebox. At the same time, other smokers tend to require minor fire with fewer coals and a completely different combination of the vent and draw controls. However, most smokers are designed to work at temperatures as low as 180 degrees Fahrenheit to as high as 300 degrees Fahrenheit. But the recommended temperature usually falls between 250 degrees Fahrenheit and 275 degrees Fahrenheit.
- **AIRFLOW:** The air to which the fire is significantly exposed determines how your fire will burn and how quickly it will burn the fuel. For instance, if you restrict airflow into the firebox by closing up the available vents, the fire will burn at a low temperature and vice versa. Typically in smokers, after lighting up the fire, the vents are opened to allow for maximum airflow and are then adjusted throughout the cooking process to ensure that optimum flame is achieved.
- **INSULATION:** Insulation is also essential for smokers as it helps to manage the cooking process throughout the whole cooking session. Good insulation allows smokers to reach the desired temperature instead of waiting hours!

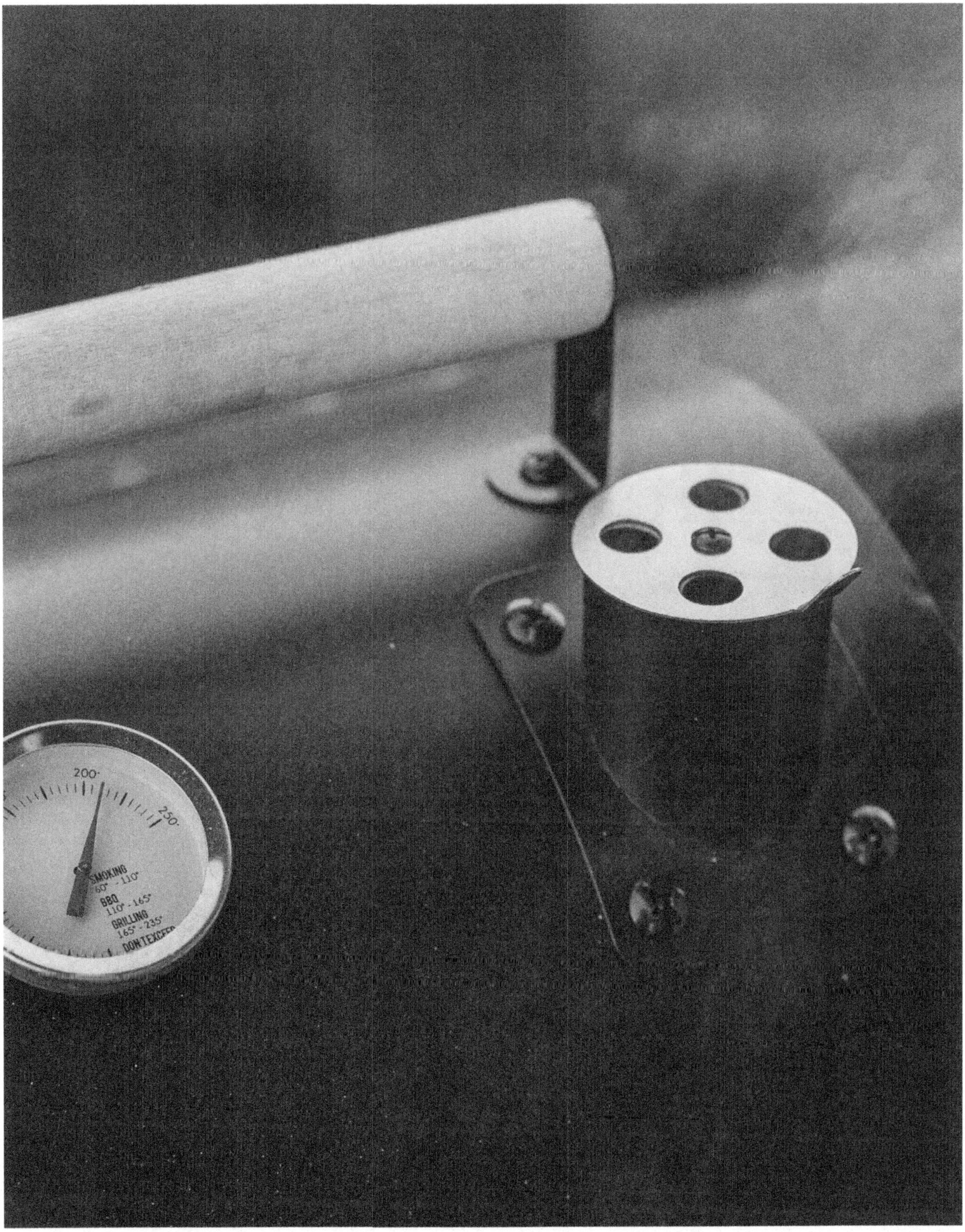
200°
250°
SMOKING
60° - 110°
BBQ
110° - 165°
GRILLING
165° - 235°

CHAPTER 8

FOOD SAFETY

CLEANLINESS OF THE MEAT 104
KEEPING YOUR MEAT COLD 105
KEEPING YOUR MEAT COVERED...107
PREVENTING FORMS OF
CROSS-CONTAMINATION 108
KNIVES 108

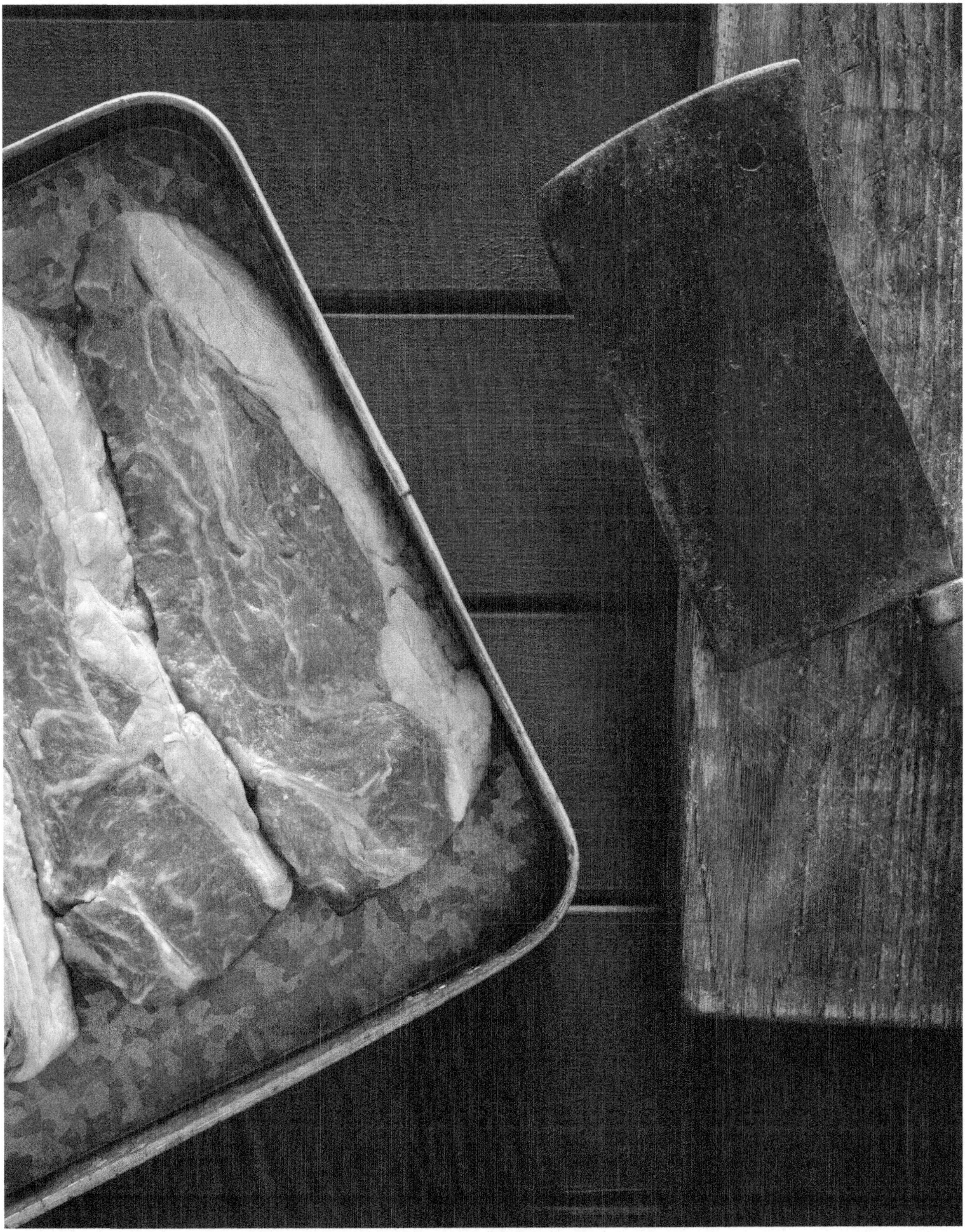

CLEANLINESS OF THE MEAT

If you can follow the steps below, you will be able to ensure that your meat is safe from any bacterial or airborne contamination.

This first step is essential as no market-bought or freshly cut meat is entirely sterile.

Following these would significantly minimize the risk of getting affected by diseases.

- Make sure to properly wash your hands before beginning to process your meat. Use fresh tap water and soap/hand sanitizer.
- Make sure to remove metal ornaments such as rings and watches from your wrist and hand before handling the meat.
- Thoroughly clean the cutting surface using sanitizing liquid to remove any grease or unwanted contaminants. If you want a homemade sanitizer, you can simply make a solution of 1 part chlorine bleach and ten parts water.
- The sanitizer mentioned above should also be used to soak your tools, such as knives and other equipment, to ensure that they are safe to use.
- Alternatively, commercial acid based/ no rinsed sanitizers such as Star San will also work.
- After each use, all knives and other equipment, such as meat grinders, slicers, extruders, etc., should be cleaned thoroughly using soap water. The knives should be taken care in particular by cleaning the place just on top of the handle as it might contain blood and pieces of meat.
- When cleaning the surface, you should use cloths or sponges.

A note of sponges/clothes: It is ideal that you keep your sponge or cleaning cloth clean as it might result in cross-contamination. These are ideal harboring places for foodborne pathogens. Just follow the simple steps to ensure that you are on the safe side:
- Make sure to clean your sponge daily. It is seen that the effectiveness of cleaning it increases if you microwave the dam sponge for 1 minute and disinfect it using a solution of ¼ -1/2 teaspoon of concentrated bleach. This process will kill 99% of bacteria.
- Replace your sponge frequently, as using the same sponge every time (even with wash) will result in eventual bacterial growth.
- When not using the sponge, please keep it dry and wring it off of any loose food or debris.

KEEPING YOUR MEAT COLD

Mismanagement of temperature is one of the most common reasons for outbreaks of foodborne diseases. The study has shown that bacteria grow best at temperatures of 40 to 140 degree Fahrenheit/4-60 degree Celsius, which means that if not taken care of properly, bacteria in the meat will start to multiply very quickly. The best way to prevent this is to keep your meat cold before using it. Keep them eat in your fridge before processing them and make sure that the temperature is below 40 degrees Fahrenheit/4 degree Celsius.

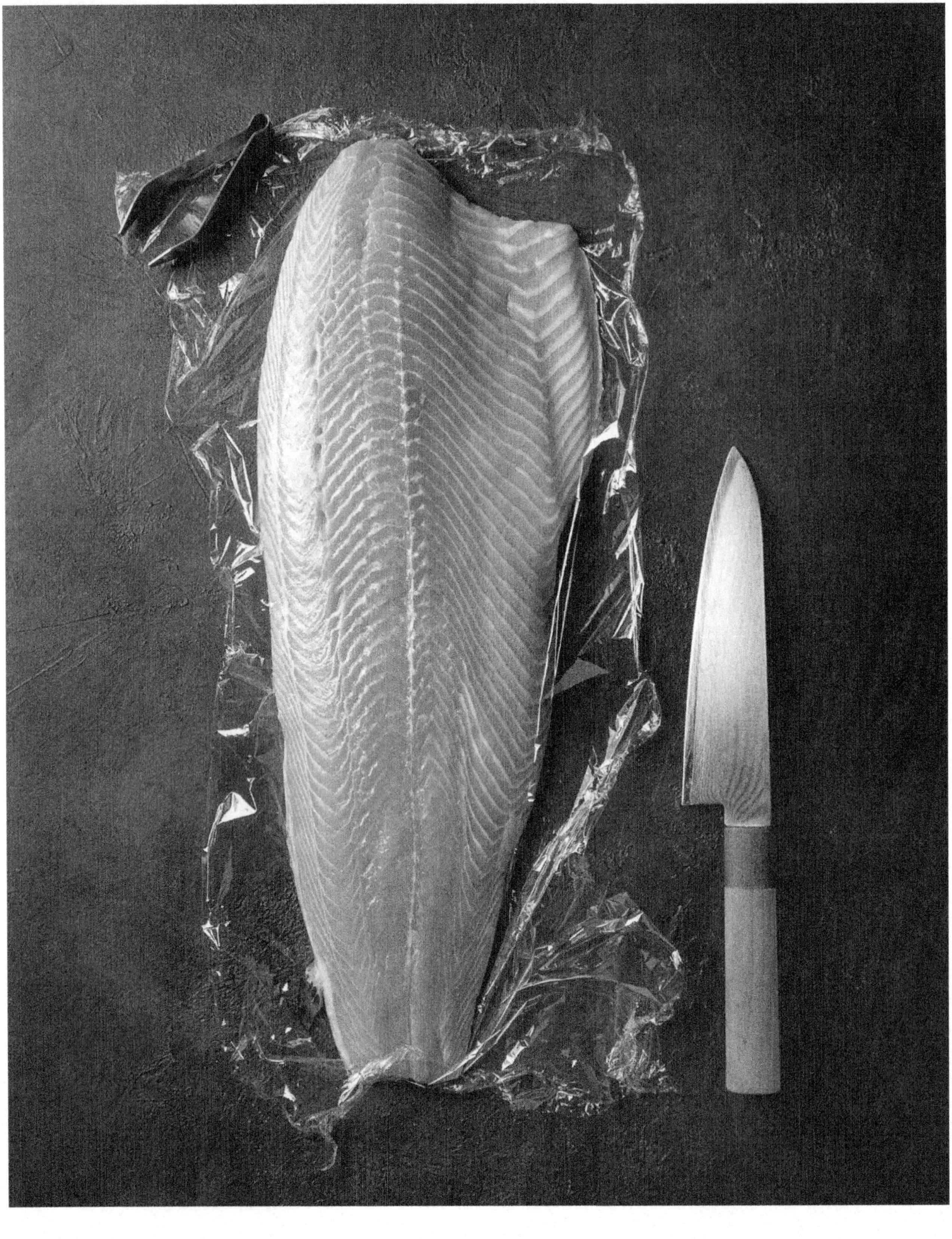

KEEPING YOUR MEAT COVERED

All foods start to diminish once they are opened from their packaging or exposed to the air. However, the effect can be greatly minimized if you cover or wrap the foods properly.

The same goes for meat.

Good ways of keeping your meat covered and wrapped include:

- Using aluminum foil to cover up your meat will help to protect it from light and oxygen and keep the moisture intact. However, since Aluminum is reactive, it is advised that a layer of plastic wrap is used underneath the aluminum foil to provide a double protective coating.
- If the meat is kept in a bowl with no lid, then plastic wrap can seal the bowl, providing an airtight enclosure.
- Re-sealable bags protect by storing them in a bag and squeezing out any air.
- Airtight glass or plastic containers with lids are good options as well.
- A type of paper known as Freezer paper is specifically designed to wrap foods to be kept in the fridge. These wraps are excellent for meat as well.
- Vacuum sealers are often used for Sous Vide packaging. These machines are a bit expensive but can provide excellent packaging by completely sucking out any air from a re-sealable bag. This greatly increases the meat's shelf life outside and in the fridge.

PREVENTING FORMS OF CROSS-CONTAMINATION

Cross-Contamination usually occurs when one food comes into contact with another. In our case, we are talking about our meats.

This can be avoided very easily by keeping the following things in check:
- Always wash your hands thoroughly with warm water. The cutting boards, counters, knives, and other utensils should also be cleaned as instructed in the chapter's first section.
- Keep different types of meat in separate bowls, dishes, and plates before using them.
- When storing the meat in the fridge, keep the raw meat, seafood, poultry, and eggs on the bottom shelf of your fridge and in individual sealed containers.
- Keep your refrigerator shelves cleaned, and juices from meat/vegetables might drip on them.
- Always refrain from keeping raw meat/vegetables on the same plate as cooked goods.
- Always clean your cutting boards and use different cutting boards for different foods. Raw meats, vegetables, and other foods should be cut using a different table.

KNIVES

Knives: Sharp knives should be used to slice the meat accordingly. While using the knife, you should keep the following in mind.
- Always make sure to use a sharp knife
- Never hold a knife under your arm or leave it under a piece of meat
- Always keep your knives within visible distance
- Always keep your knife point down
- Always cut down towards the cutting surface and away from your body
- Never allow children to toy with knives unattended
- Wash the knives while cutting different types of food

Recipes Index

A

ALDER SMOKED APPLE CIDER SALMON, 12
APPLE SMOKED TILAPIA WITH GINGER AND GRAPEFRUIT MARINADE, 62
APRICOT SMOKED SALMON, 13
ASIAN COHO SMOKED SALMON, 15
ASIAN ORANGE AND TUNA SALAD, 36

B

BACON-WRAPPED SHRIMP AND CRAB BITES, 48
BARBECUING AND SMOKING MEAT, 90
BASIC PREPARATIONS, 99
BASTE FOR GRILLED FISH, 84
BROWN SUGAR SMOKED SALMON, 19

C

CAJUN SMOKED CATFISH, 63
CHARCOAL, 97
CHOOSE YOUR WOOD, 95
CITRUS MARINATED SCALLOPS, 49
CITRUS STUFFED RAINBOW TROUT WITH BROWN BUTTER, 23
CLEANLINESS OF THE MEAT, 104
COLD AND HOT SMOKING, 91
CREAMY SMOKED OYSTER SPREAD, 51

D

DIFFERENT SMOKER STYLES, 94
DIFFERENT SMOKER TYPES, 93

E

ELEMENTS OF SMOKING, 100

F

FRESH TROUT, CREAM CHEESE, AND RED ONION BAGUETTE, 28

G

GARLIC BUTTER LOBSTER TAILS, 52

H

HOISIN AND ORANGE SMOKED TILAPIA, 65
HONEY LIME MARINADE FOR SALMON, 79
HONEY LIME SMOKED SNAPPER, 66
HOT AND SPICY TUNA, 37
HOT SMOKED KINGFISH, 67

K

KEEPING YOUR MEAT COLD, 105
KEEPING YOUR MEAT COVERED, 107
KING CRAB LEGS IN LEMON BUTTER, 55
KNIVES, 108

L

LEMON AND DILL SALMON SEASONING, 78
LEMON BUTTER SAUCE, 81
LEMON-PEPPER AHI TUNA STEAKS, 39
LITTLENECK SMOKED CLAMS, 56

M

MAHI MAHI WITH CORN AND WATERMELON SALAD, 69
MAPLE AND ORANGE SMOKED SALMON, 20
MAPLE SMOKED SMELT, 71
MAPLE-SMOKED TUNA, 40

O

ORANGE-SAGE RUB FOR MEAT, POULTRY, AND FISH, 85

P

PECAN SMOKED SHRIMP WITH BOOZY BBQ SAUCE, 54
PESTO TOPPED SALMON, 16
PREVENTING FORMS OF CROSS-CONTAMINATION, 108

R

RIGHT TEMPERATURE, 98

S

SELECTING A SMOKER, 92
SHRIMP COCKTAIL, 58
SMOKED CATFISH WITH A HERB MARINADE, 72
SMOKED HALIBUT IN A TANGERINE AND HOISIN SAUCE GLAZE, 74
SMOKED RAINBOW TROUT WITH BROWN SUGAR, 24
SMOKED RAINBOW TROUT WITH LEMON DILL SAUCE, 33
SMOKED SALMON NUGGETS, 17
SMOKED TROUT WITH BEET AND POTATO HASH, 26
SMOKED TROUT WITH GARLIC, LEMON, AND BASIL, 30
SMOKED TROUT WITH GREEK FETA SALAD, 31
SMOKED WHITE WINE MUSSELS, 59
SMOKEY TUNA TACOS, 43
SPICY PINK GRAPEFRUIT AND HERB MARINADE FOR FISH, 82, 87
SWORDFISH IN LEMON AND OLIVE OIL, 75

T

THAI TUNA FISHCAKES, 42
TUNA STEAKS, 45

CONCLUSION

I am happy to share this cookbook with you, and I take pride in offering you an extensive array of recipes that you will love and enjoy. I hope you benefit from each of our recipes, and I am sure you will like all the recipes we have offered you. Don't hesitate to try our creative and easy-to-make recipes, and remember that I have put my heart into coming up with delicious meals for you. If you like my recipes, you can share them with acquaintances and friends. I need your encouragement to continue writing more books!

P.S. Thank you for reading this book. If you've enjoyed this book, please don't shy; drop me a line, leave feedback, or both on Amazon. I love reading feedback and your opinion is extremely important to me.

COPYRIGHT 2022© ROGER MURPHY

All rights reserved. No part of this guide may be reproduced in any form without permission in writing from the publisher except in the case of brief quotations embodied in critical articles or reviews.

Legal & Disclaimer: The information contained in this book and its contents is not designed to replace or take the place of any form of medical or professional advice; and is not meant to replace the need for independent medical, financial, legal, or other professional advice or services, as may be required. The content and information in this book have been provided for educational and entertainment purposes only. The content and information in this book have been compiled from reliable sources, and it is accurate to the best of the Author's knowledge, information, and belief. However, the Author cannot guarantee its accuracy and validity and cannot be held liable for errors and omissions. Further, changes are periodically made to this book as and when needed. Therefore, where appropriate and necessary, you must consult a professional (including but not limited to your doctor, attorney, financial advisor, or such other professional advisor) before using any of the suggested remedies, techniques, or information in this book.

Upon using the contents and information in this book, you agree to hold harmless the Author from and against any damages, costs, and expenses, including any legal fees potentially resulting from the application of any of the information provided.

This disclaimer applies to any loss, damages, or injury caused by the use and application, whether directly or indirectly, of any advice or information presented, whether for breach of contract, tort, negligence, personal injury, criminal intent, or under any other cause of action.

You agree to accept all risks of using the information presented in this book. You agree that by continuing to read this book, where appropriate and necessary, you shall consult a professional (including but not limited to your doctor, attorney, financial advisor, or such other advisor as needed) before using any of the suggested remedies, techniques, or information in this book.